Who Really Killed JFK?

(Facts & Theories)

Introduction

John Fitzgerald Kennedy, the thirty-fifth President of the United States, was assassinated at 12:30 pm Central Standard Time on Friday, November 22, 1963, in Dealey Plaza, Dallas, Texas. Kennedy was fatally shot while traveling with his wife Jacqueline, Texas Governor John Connally, and the latter's wife, Nellie, in a Presidential Motorcade. The ten-month investigation of the Warren Commission of 1963–1964 concluded that the President was assassinated by Lee Harvey Oswald acting alone and that Jack Ruby acted alone when he killed Oswald before he could stand Trial. These conclusions were initially supported by the American public; however, polls conducted from 1966 to 2004 found that as many as 80 percent of Americans have suspected that there was a plot or cover-up.

Contrary to the Warren Commission, the United States House Select Committee on Assassinations (HSCA) in 1979 concluded that President John F. Kennedy was probably assassinated as a result of a conspiracy. The HSCA found both the original FBI investigation and the Warren Commission Report to be seriously flawed. While agreeing with the Commission that Oswald fired all the shots which caused the wounds to Kennedy and Governor Connally, it stated that there were at least four shots fired and that there was a "high probability" that two gunmen fired at the President. No gunmen or groups involved in the conspiracy were identified by the committee, but the CIA, Soviet Union, Organized Crime and several other groups were said to be not involved, based on available evidence. The assassination is still the subject of widespread debate and has spawned numerous conspiracy theories and alternative scenarios.

I do not know who planned the assassination, nor who fired the shots. But I am convinced there was a conspiracy. This book is about John F. Kennedy visit to Texas in 1963 and the detailed timeline of events before, during, and after his assassination.

Chapters includes: Timeline of Kennedy Assassination, Fatal Day Players, Photos of the Crime Scene, Dealey Plaza Witnesses, Who Really Killed JFK? A New View of Old Evidence, JFK Legacy, JFK Funeral, JFK Last Speech in Ft. Worth and CIA Director withheld information about JFK.

Therlee Gipson (updated February 14, 2016)

Compiled 2015
by Therlee Gipson

ISBN- 978-1519405333

Table of Contents

	Page No.
Title of Book………………………………………………………………	1
Prelude, Copyright………………………………………………………	2
Table of Contents………………………………………………………	3–6

Chapter I

Timeline of Kennedy's Assassination…………………………………	7 – 20
• 11:40 am CST, Friday, November 22, 1963………………………	8
• Dealey Plaza the afternoon of November 22, 1963………………	9
• Moments before the assassination began…………………………	10
• Immediate aftermath…………………………………………………	11
• The is the rifle Oswald used to kill JFK…………………………..	12
• Parkland Hospital after Kennedy's assassination…………………	13
• Officer Tippit murder………………………………………………..	14
• Walter Cronkite announce Kennedy's death………………………	15
• Texas Theater…………………………………………………………	16
• Bird eye view of Dealey Plaza and Oak Cliff:……………………	17
• Lyndon B. Johnson sworn in Office………………………………..	18
• Kennedy body returned to Washington D.C………………………	19
• Oswald held News Conference……………………………………..	20

Chapter II

Fatal Day Players……………………………………………………….	21–36
• **Sarah Tilghman Hughes**…………………………………………	22
• **Lyndon Baines Johnson** …………………………………………	23, 24
• **John Bowden Connally, Jr.** ……………………………………	25
• **Lee Harvey Oswald**………………………………………………	26–33
• **Jack Ruby**…………………………………………………………..	34
• **J. D. Tippit** ………………………………………………………..	35
• **John F. Kennedy**……………………………………………………	36

Table of Contents

Page No.

Chapter III

Photos of the Tragic Event in Dallas.. 37 – 48
- Dealey Plaza the afternoon of November 22, 1963.................................. 38
- The Texas Schoolbook Depository (Where the three shots were fired from)........ 39
- Texas School Book Depository Building... 40
- Fifth and Sixth floors taken shortly after the assassination........................ 41
- Arrows indicate spent shell casing on floor on November 25, 1963................ 42
- Position of boxes in window on November 25, 1963................................. 43
- Position of boxes in window and rifle he used, on November 25, 1963............ 44
- Oswald's mug shot and finger prints... 45
- Oswald bought rifle into the Depository concealed in a long paper bag............ 46
- Oswald's arrest and death.. 47
- The boarding house where Oswald rented and his room............................ 48

Chapter IV

Dealey Plaza Witnesses... 49–66
- Abraham Zapruder... 50
- Roger Craig; Seymour Weitzman.. 51
- Marilyn Sitzman; Julia Ann Mercer... 52
- Jean Hill; Tom Tilson; Phil Willis; Jackie Kennedy; Rufus Youngblood.... 53
- Texas Monthly Witnesses; Ed Hoffman.. 54
- Gordon Arnold 55
- Lee Bowers... 56, 57
- Charles F. Brehm.. 58, 59
- James M. Chaney; William Greer.. 60, 61
- William "Billy" Allen Harper... 62
- Jean Lollis Hill 63
- Roy Kellerman... 64
- Different Ads to welcome President John F. Kennedy............................. 65, 66

Table of Contents

Page No.

Chapter V

Who Really Killed JFK? .... 67 – 80

- **17 Theories** on Who Killed JFK 68
- Where Did the Term "Grassy Knoll" Come From? The Umbrella Man 69
- **Theory No. 1**: Lee Harvey Oswald 70, 71
- **Theory No. 2**: The Mafia 72
- **Theory No. 3**: The Soviet Union 73
- **Theory No. 4**: Right-Wing Activists in New Orleans 73
- **Theory No. 5**: Antoine Guerini and the Marseilles Mafia 74
- **Theory No. 6**: Lyndon B. Johnson and Texas Oil Millionaires 74
- **Theory No. 7**: David Atlee Phillips and the CIA 75
- **Theory No. 8**: Rogue Members of the CIA 75
- **Theory No. 9**: Jack Ruby and the Mafia 76
- **Theory No. 10**: E. Howard Hunt and the CIA 76
- **Theory No. 11**: The Mafia, Anti-Castro Activists and the CIA 77
- **Theory No. 12**: CIA and Executive Action 77
- **Theory No. 13**: Secret Service Conspiracy 78
- **Theory No. 14**: J. Edgar Hoover and the FBI 78
- **Theory No. 15**: John Birch Society 79
- **Theory No 16**: The Three Tramps 79
- **Theory No 17**: Anti Integration Group 80

Chapter VI

A New View of Old Evidence 81–84

- Grassy Knoll Shooter: Blowing Smoke 82
- The Smell of "Gunpowder" in the Plaza 83
- A Secret Service Man on the Knoll? 83
- Acoustic Evidence of Four Shots? 84
- The Limo Slowed When the Shooting Started 84
- The Babushka Lady 84

Table of Contents

Page No.

Chapter VII

JFK Legacy... 85 – 91
- Television coverage gave us information................................... 86
- Political and historical importance.. 87
- Civil Rights.. 87, 88
- John F. Kennedy Quotes... 89
- The Kennedy Tragedies... 90
- Chronology... 90, 91

Presidents Assassinated in Office... 92

Chapter VIII

JFK Funeral.. 93–100
- President Kennedy casket... 94
- Pennsylvania Avenue.. 95
- Leader of the Nation supporting the Kennedy family................. 96
- First burial site and Church service of John F. Kennedy............ 97
- Kennedy wife accept his flag; Kennedy final resting place........ 98, 99
- Honors to John F. Kennedy.. 100

Chapter IX

JFK Last Speech in Ft. Worth... 101–107
- JFK's Last Night at Hotel Texas 1963 Fort Worth, TX................ 102, 103
- The morning of November 22, 1963.. 104
- Speaking to crowds; JFK Memorial in Ft. Worth........................ 105–107

The 50th: Honoring the Memory of JFK Unspoken Speech in Dallas............. 108

Chapter X

CIA Director withheld information about JFK........................ 109–114
- Oswald's Raleigh Call... 115–117
- **10 Fact about Kennedy Death**... 118–121
- **Walking Tour of Dealey Plaza**.. 122, 123

Acknowledgement; (*)Source; Public Domain; Contents Disclaimer........... 124

Chapter 1

Timeline of Kennedy's Assassination

Timeline of Kennedy Assassination:

Kennedy, his wife Jacqueline, and the rest of the presidential entourage arrived at Love Field in Dallas, Texas, aboard Air Force One after a very short flight from nearby Ft. Worth. The motorcade cars had been lined up in a certain order earlier that morning but, just prior to Kennedy's arrival, the order of the vehicles was changed.

The original schedule was for the President to proceed in a long motorcade from Love Field through downtown Dallas, and end at the Dallas Business and Trade Mart.

The motorcade was scheduled to enter Dealey Plaza at 12:25 pm, followed by a 12:30 pm arrival at the Dallas Business and Trade Mart so President Kennedy could deliver a speech and share in a steak luncheon with Dallas government, business, religious, and civic leaders and their spouses.

The presidential motorcade traveled nearly its entire route without incident, stopping twice so President Kennedy could shake hands with some Catholic nuns, then, some school children. Shortly before the limousine turned onto Main Street a male ran towards the limousine, but was thrust to the ground by a Secret Service agent and hustled away. (cont.)

Dealey Plaza the afternoon of November 22, 1963:

12:29 pm CST, the Presidential limousine entered Dealey Plaza after a 90-degree right turn from Main Street onto Houston Street. Over two dozen known and unknown amateur and professional still and motion-picture photographers captured the last living images of President Kennedy.

Just before 12:30 pm CST, President Kennedy slowly approached the Texas School Book Depository head-on, then the limousine slowly made the 120-degree left turn directly in front of the depository, now only 65 feet (20 meters) away. The assassination began when the Presidential limousine had completed the slowing turn, and glided down the three-degree inclined Elm Street to a point level with the Southwest corner of the Depository. President Kennedy was targeted and shot at for an estimated 6 to 9 seconds. He was hit with at least two bullets, and was killed when struck in his head, (cont.)

Moments before the assassination began

Notice all the protection around the limousine following the President's Limousine

The first car in the convoy, known as the "Pilot Car," carried Dallas Police Officers. It stayed a quarter-mile ahead of the political parade that followed and was assigned to report signs of trouble. Next came six motorcycles, then the "Lead Car," an unmarked Dallas police vehicle driven by Police Chief Police Jesse Curry and occupied by Dallas County Sheriff Bill Decker and Secret Service Agents Forrest Sorrels, of the White House detail, and Winston Lawson, special Agent in charge of the Dallas office.

In Downtown Dallas, the Motorcade slowed to 10 mph as the Kennedys and Connallys smiled and waved to the masses lining the route, a crowd estimated at two hundred and fifty thousands. At Houston Street, the Motorcade turned right off Main, then left onto Elm to allow quick passage through Dealey Plaza for the final leg of the trip. As the Motorcade moved toward the Texas Schoolbook Depository building, Nellie Connally turned and remarked about the greeting that the Kennedys were receiving. The Governor's wife said, "*Mr. President, you can't say that Dallas doesn't love you.*" , "*That is very obvious.*" These were John Kennedy's last words. (cont.)

Immediate aftermath:

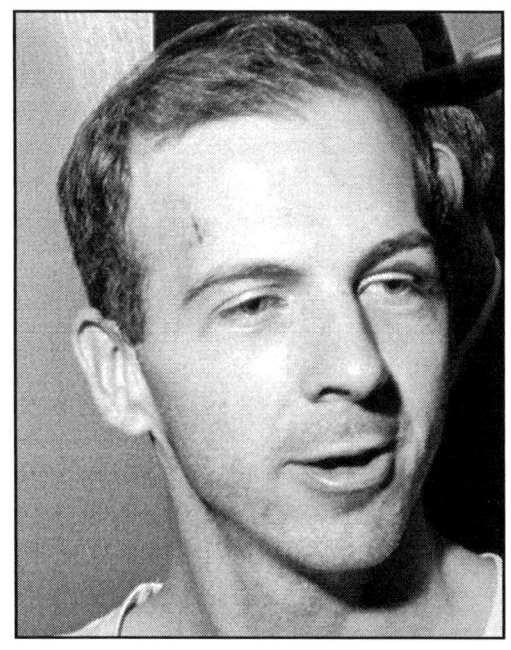

Lee Harvey Oswald was confronted by an armed Dallas Policeman, Marion Baker, in the depository second floor lunchroom only 74 to 90 seconds (according to a Warren Commission time recreation) after the last shot. Baker first testified that the shots he remembered hearing as he approached the depository originated from the "*building in front of me, or, the one to the right*". In the second floor lunchroom Oswald was identified by the superintendent of the building, Roy Truly, then released. Both Baker and Truly testified that Oswald appeared completely "*calm, cool, normal, and was not out of breath in any way*" and was not sweating.

Oswald's possible escape route used The light-colored Rambler station wagon (see bottom photo) that was seen with someone who was practically a double for Lee Harvey Oswald passed under the Triple Underpass at 12:40 pm.

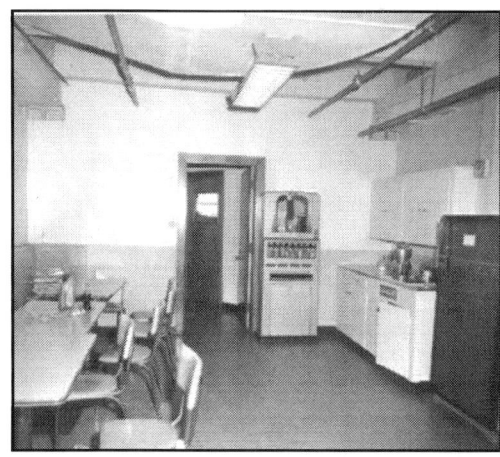

A few blocks beyond that overpass is the Commerce Street Viaduct, leading directly into Oak Cliff. It is practically certain that after the Rambler with an unknown driver and a "Oswald impostor" left the Depository it crossed the viaduct, and after turning left on Sylvan Street drove 12 blocks further going South on Davis St. (cont.)

The is the rifle Oswald used to kill JFK:

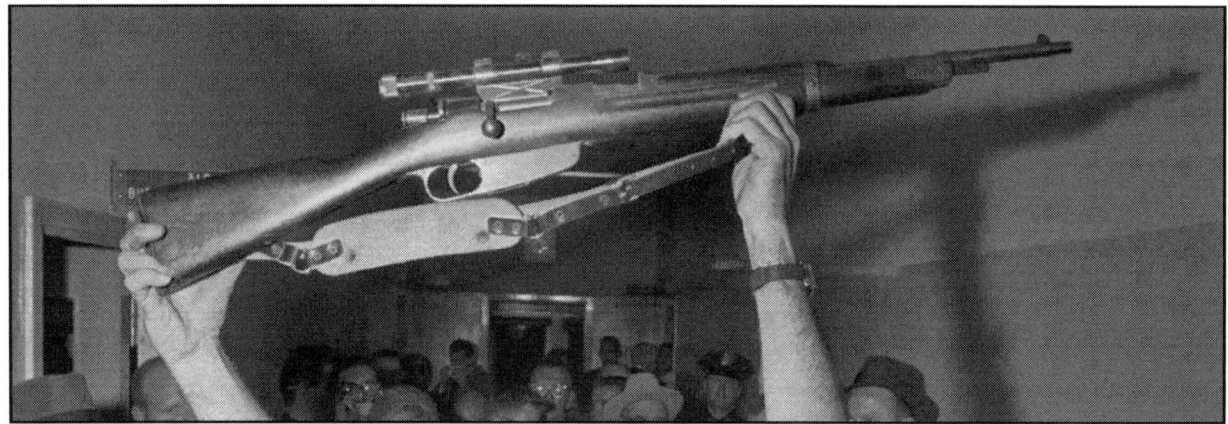

This is a Mannlicher-Carcano 6.5mm bolt-action rifle, the M91 Cavalry Carbine variant. The Mannlicher-Carcano is most famous as the gun that was allegedly used by Lee Harvey Oswald to shoot John F. Kennedy. Who really picked up the rifle?

The Warren Commission concluded that Oswald had traveled a minimum 346 foot distance from the sixth floor easternmost window, and hid an 8 pound, 1938-Italian made Mannlicher-Carcano, 6.5 millimeter rifle equipped with a four-power scope along the way. The rifle was reported discovered by a Dallas Police Detective at 1:22 pm, having been placed sometime sitting balanced upright on its bottom edges. After being discovered the rifle was photographed before being touched.

Authorities did not seal the Texas School Book Depository until 12:39 or 12:40 pm. Before that, Policemen, Detectives, witnesses, and others were first directed by persons to search the Grassy Knoll, parking lot, and railroad yard from 12:30 to 12:39 pm. The Dealey Plaza immediate area Streets and blocks were never sealed-off either, and within only nine minutes of the assassination, photographs show that vehicles were driving down Elm Street, through the crime scene kill zone.

At 1:00 pm, after a bus and taxi ride (a taxi ride that he was witnessed offering first to an elderly woman), Oswald arrived back at his boarding room and according to his landlady, left at 1:03 or 1:04 pm when she last saw him standing and waiting at a bus stop. (cont.)

Parkland Hospital after Kennedy's assassination:

At 1:00 pm CST:
After all the heart activity had ceased, and after the Priest administered the last rites, President Kennedy was pronounced dead. Personnel at Parkland Hospital trauma room #1 who treated the President observed that the President's condition was "moribund", meaning, he had no chance of survival upon arrival at the Hospital.

Meanwhile, the situation at Parkland Hospital (see upper photo) had deteriorated. Even as the Press contingent grew, a Roman Catholic Priest had been summoned to perform the last rites for President Kennedy. Doctors worked frantically to save his life, but his wounds were too great. *"We never had any hope of saving his life,"*

one Doctor said. The Priest who administered the last rites to the President told **The New York Times** that the President was already dead upon arrival at the Hospital and had to draw back a sheet covering the President's face so that the last rites could be given. Governor Connally, meanwhile, was soon taken to emergency surgery where he underwent two operations that day. (cont.)

Officer Tippit murder:

At 1:15 to 1:16 pm

(one nearby witness who actually looked at his watch stated 1:10 pm), Dallas Police Officer J. D. Tippit (see photo on your left) was shot dead 0.88 miles from Oswald's rooming house. Nine people witnessed Oswald either shooting Tippit or fleeing the immediate scene. Two witnesses stated they saw another man near Oswald at the killing site. The very closest witness to the shooting (only 34 feet away) first refused to identify Oswald as the Tippit killer (and only identified Oswald after his brother was shot in the head in a bar in January 1964). After the Tippit murder, Oswald was witnessed traveling on foot toward the Texas Theatre.

At about 1:35 pm

Johnny Calvin Brewer (see bottom photo), who worked as a manager at "**Hardy's Shoe Store**" nearby the "**Texas Theatre**" saw Oswald turning his face away from the Street and duck into the entranceway of the shoe store as Dallas squad cars sirened up the Street. When Oswald left the store,

Brewer followed Oswald and watched him go into the Texas Theater movie house without paying while the ticket attendant was distracted. Brewer notified the ticket taker, who in turn informed the Dallas Police at 1:40 pm.

Inside the theater, several witnesses saw Oswald shift to several different seat locations to sit next to different patrons. Speculation about Oswald's behavior in the Texas Theater has been theorized as an attempt to meet with a conspirator in order to obtain documents and funds to facilitate Oswald's escape, though he could also simply have been avoiding detection on the Street. (cont.)

Walter Cronkite announce Kennedy's death:

At 1:38 pm CST:

The news of Kennedy's death was made public. *CBS News* anchorman Walter Cronkite (see photo on left) passed along word of the assassination.

The Television transmissions had been first interrupted at 12:40 pm CST, nearly an hour before the death announcement, after which regular programming was briefly resumed. Walter Cronkite (read several more news reports and then, around 1 pm CST, the affiliates joined Cronkite in the news room. After news footage was shown of a luncheon in Dallas where Kennedy was supposed to speak, (see his empty chair) Cronkite announced on air:

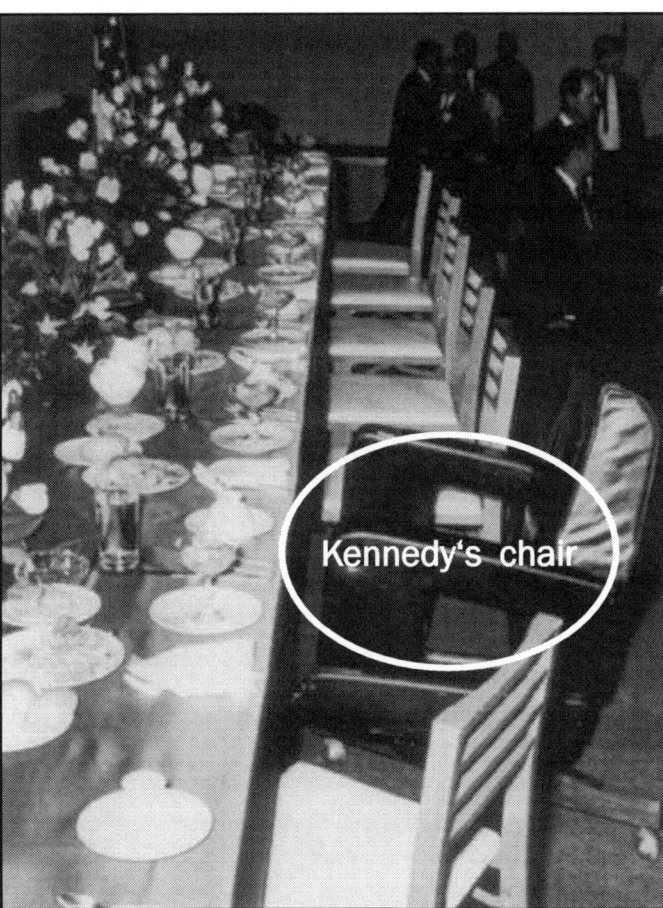

"From Dallas, Texas, the flash, apparently official--(reading AP flash) President Kennedy died at 1:00 pm Central Standard Time, 2:00 Eastern Standard Time, some 38 minutes ago. Vice President Lyndon Johnson has left the hospital in Dallas, but we do not know to where he has proceeded. Presumably, he will be taking the Oath of Office shortly and become the thirty-sixth President of the United States." (cont.)

Oswald apprehended at Texas Theater

Almost two dozen Policemen, Sheriffs, and detectives in several patrol cars arrived at Texas Theatre because they believed Tippit's killer was inside. (Minutes beforehand they had raided a nearby Library on a similar, but mistaken report.) When an arrest attempt was made at 1:50 pm inside the Theater, Oswald resisted arrest and, according to the Police, attempted to shoot a patrolman after yelling once, "*Well, it's all over now!*" then punching a patrolman. A Policeman was witnessed to immediately yell, "*Kill the President, will 'ya?!!*"

As a commemoration to the historic capture, the words "Lee Harvey Oswald, November 22, 1963" were later painted in gold paint on the chair Oswald (supposedly) occupied (the actual chair was removed by the then, manager "Butch" Burroughs who took it home and replaced it with another one which the FBI confiscated the next day for evidence thinking it was the original. (*)

(*) Source: (see page 124)

Map bird eye view of Dealey Plaza and Oak Cliff:

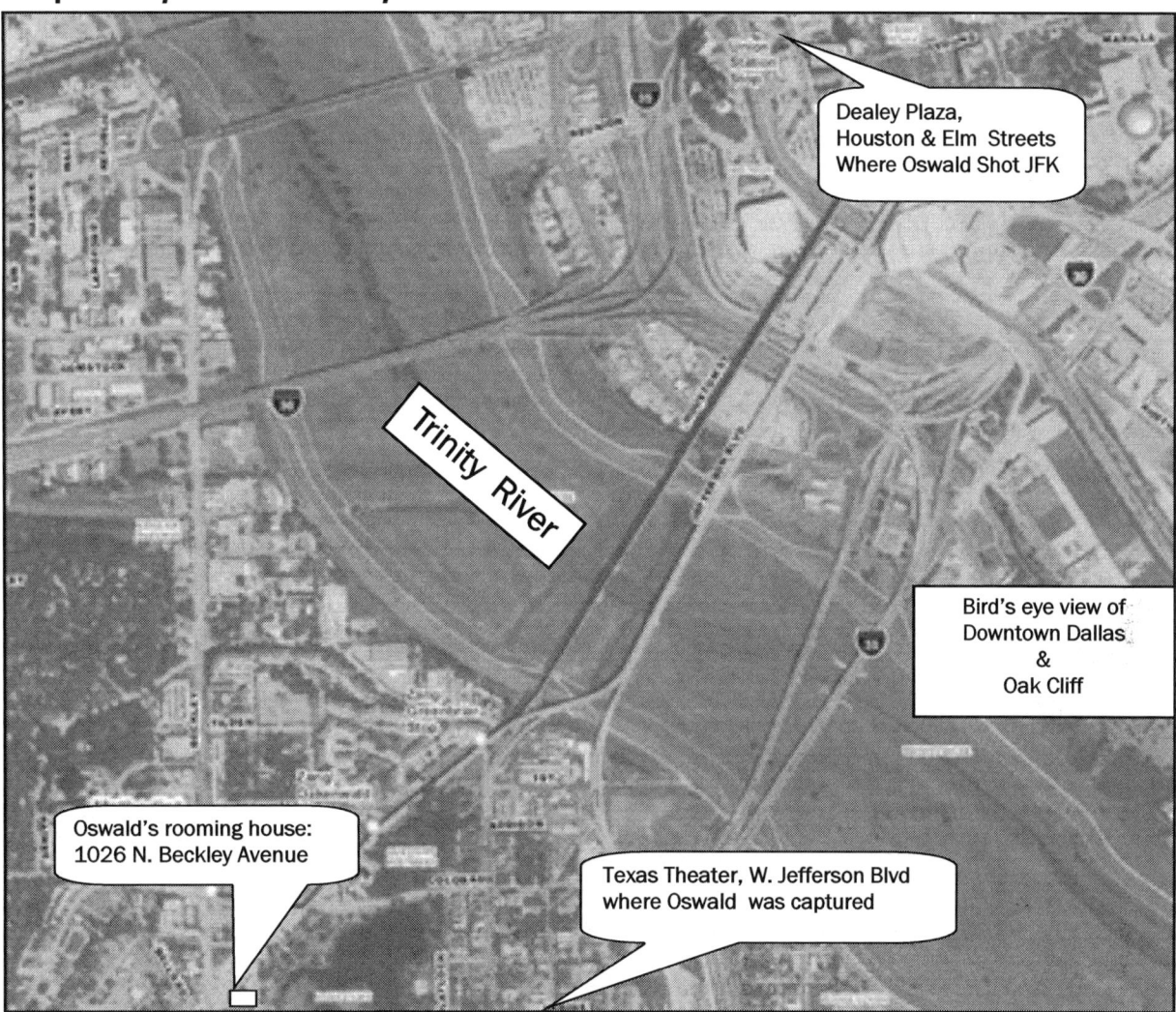

Texas Theater is located at 231 West Jefferson Boulevard in the Oak Cliff neighborhood of Dallas, Texas. It gained Historical fame for being the place Lee Harvey Oswald, the alleged assassin of President John F. Kennedy and Dallas police officer J. D. Tippit, was arrested after a brief fight. Oswald's rooming house was located at 1026 N. Beckley, not far from Texas Theater.

After the fatal shooting of Officer Tippit at approximately 1:16 pm, Oswald entered the Texas Theater shortly after 1:30 pm without paying for a ticket, ostensibly to avoid police. They were later informed by the assistant manager that a man had entered the theater without paying. The films being presented on that day were *Cry of Battle* and *War Is Hell*. Oswald briefly viewed the latter. Today, Texas Theater hosts a Repertory Cinema and special events. (*)

(*) Source: (see page 124)

Lyndon B. Johnson sworn in Office:

2:00 pm CST: A few minutes after and after a ten to fifteen minute confrontation between cursing and weapons-brandishing Secret Service Agents and Doctors, President Kennedy's body was illegally removed from Parkland Hospital and driven to Air Force One. The body was removed before undergoing a forensic examination by the Dallas coroner, and against Texas State Laws (the murder of the President was a State crime, and legally occurred under Texas jurisdiction.

At 2:38 pm CST, after Mrs. Kennedy and President Kennedy's body had also returned to Air Force One, Lyndon Johnson was sworn in as the thirty-sixth President of the United States of America. (cont.)

Kennedy body returned to Washington D.C.:

At about 6:00 pm EST:

Air Force One arrived at Andrews Air Force Base near Washington D.C. where Kennedy's casket was loaded into a light gray U.S. Navy ambulance for its transport to the Bethesda Naval Hospital for an autopsy and mortician's preparations. When Jackie Kennedy stepped off the plane, her pink suit and legs were still stained with her husband's blood. All that long afternoon and into the early morning hours of the next day, the widow objected to leaving her husband's body, except for the swearing in of Johnson. She also refused to change out of her blood-stained suit. "*Let them see what they've done*" she has been quoted by several persons as saying. (cont.)

Oswald held News Conference:

At 3:01 pm

Dallas time, only an hour after Oswald was taken into the Dallas Jail, FBI Director J. Edgar Hoover wrote a memo to his assistant Directors in which he stated, *"I called the Attorney General at his home and told him I thought we had the man who killed the President down in Dallas, at the present time"*.

At about 7:30 pm CST, Lee Harvey Oswald was charged with "**murder with malice**" in the killing of police officer J.D. Tippit.

At 11:36 pm CST, Oswald was charged with the murder of President Kennedy (there being no crime of "**assassination**" at that time). (cont.)

Chapter II

Fatal Day Players

(1896-1985)

Sarah Tilghman Hughes was born on August 2, 1896 in Baltimore, Maryland, she was the daughter of James and Elizabeth Haughton Tilghman. After High School at the all-girl Western High School in Baltimore, she attended Goucher College in Baltimore. After graduation she taught science at Salem Academy in North Carolina for several years. She then returned to School to the study of Law. In 1919 she moved to Washington, D.C., and attended The George Washington University Law School. She attended classes at night and during the day worked as a Police Officer. At that time she lived in a tent home near the Potomac River and commuted to the campus by canoe each evening.

She moved to Dallas, Texas in, 1922 with her husband, George Hughes, whom she had met in Law School. She practiced Law for eight years in Dallas before becoming involved in Politics, first being elected in 1930 to three Terms in the Texas House of Representatives. In 1935, she accepted an appointment as a State Judge from Governor James Allred for the Fourteenth District Court in Dallas and was the State's first woman District Judge. In 1936 she was elected to the same Post. She was re-elected six more times and remained at that Post until 1960.

As a Reward for her involvement with the Democratic Party, in 1961, President John F. Kennedy appointed her to the Federal Bench. She was the first woman to serve as a Federal District Judge in Texas. Two years later, on November 22, 1963, she was called upon to administer the Oath of Office to Lyndon B. Johnson after the assassination of President Kennedy. She was a member of the three Judge Panel that first heard the case of **Roe v. Wade**; the Panel's decision was subsequently affirmed by the Supreme Court of the United States.

Hughes retired from the active federal bench in 1975, though she continued to work as a judge with senior status until 1982. A close friend of Lyndon Johnson and his family, Hughes participated in his Inauguration in 1965, took part in the book signing of Lady Bird Johnson's White House memoirs, and participated in the dedication of the Lyndon Baines Johnson Library and Museum.

Judge Hughes died on April 23, 1985. She is buried in Sparkman Hillcrest Memorial Park in Dallas, Texas. The dress Hughes wore during the swearing in on Air Force One was donated to a Wax Museum in Grand Prairie, Texas. It was destroyed in a fire in 1988. . (*)

(*) Source: (see page 124)

(1908-1973)

Lyndon Baines Johnson was born on August 27, 1908 near Stonewall, Texas in the deep traditional segregated South not to his doings. He was first in Congress and ran on the Democratic ticket as Vice President with John F. Kennedy in 1960. He became President after the assassination of John F. Kennedy November 22, 1963.

Johnson was sworn-in as President on Air Force One in Dallas at Love Field Airport after the assassination of President Kennedy on November 22, 1963. He was sworn in by Federal Judge Sarah T. Hughes a very close friend of his family, making him the first President sworn in by a woman. Over the decades, many conspiracy theories from the fringe allege that Johnson was a co-conspirator behind the murder of John F. Kennedy. At the time of the assassination, President Kennedy had privately told confidantes, including his personal White House Secretary, Evelyn Lincoln, that he was considering replacing Johnson as Vice President on the 1964 Democratic ticket because Johnson was implicated in no fewer than four documented criminal investigations. Those four criminal investigations all disappeared after the assassination, after Johnson assumed the Presidency.

Johnson faced immediate difficulties upon his move into the White House. He felt that many of Kennedy's appointees did not respect him, and would never be loyal to him. He moved quickly to replace as much of Kennedy's staff as possible. As an exception, Johnson needed Bobby Kennedy to remain as Attorney General, even though the two men held a great animosity for each other. However, some of the difficulties were eased by the fact that he sat frequently on Cabinet and National Security Council meetings when Vice-President. In his first year, Johnson faced conflicts with everyone from Senators to speechwriters who wanted to honor "**Kennedy's Legacy**," but were reluctant to support new propositions by Johnson. (cont.)

(Johnson cont.)

Johnson used his famous charm and strong-arm tactics to push through his new policies. In 1964, upon Johnson's request, Congress passed a tax-reduction law and the Economic Opportunity Act, which was in association with the War on Poverty. Johnson also hired Jerri Whittington, the first African-American White House Secretary, and appointed Jack Valenti as his "Special Assistant".

In 1964, Johnson won the Presidency in his own right with 61 percent of the vote and the widest popular margin in American history—more than 15,000,000 votes. However, 1964 was also the year that Johnson supported the racist Democratic Delegates from Mississippi and denied the Mississippi Freedom Democratic Party seats at the 1964 Democratic National Convention in Atlantic City, New Jersey. To appease the Mississippi Freedom Democratic Party (MFDP) chaired by Dr. Aaron Henry with the intent of seating a passionate and charismatic leader of the Mississippi Freedom Movement, Fannie Lou Hamer, the Democrats at the convention offered the MFDP an unsatisfactory compromise and the MFDP rejected it rather than appear conciliatory in the eyes of their "comrades".

In the same year, Johnson lost the popular vote to Republican challenger Barry Goldwater in the Deep South States of Louisiana, Alabama, Mississippi, Georgia and South Carolina, a Region that had voted for Democrats since the Reconstruction era. The election, though a success for the Democratic Party, marked the beginning of the long transformation of the Democrats' Solid South to a Republican bastion.

The Great Society program became Johnson's agenda for Congress in January 1965: aid to education, attack on disease, Medicare, urban renewal, beautification, conservation, development of depressed regions, a wide-scale fight against poverty, control and prevention of crime and delinquency, removal of obstacles to the right to vote. Congress, at times augmenting or amending, rapidly enacted Johnson's recommendations. Millions of elderly people found succor through the 1965 Medicare amendment to the **Social Security Act**.

Under Johnson, the Country made spectacular explorations of space in a program he had championed since its start. When three astronauts successfully orbited the moon in December 1968, Johnson congratulated them: *"You've taken ... all of us, all over the world, into a new era...."* Nevertheless, two overriding crises had been gaining momentum since 1965. Despite the beginning of new anti-poverty and anti-discrimination programs, unrest and rioting in Black ghettos troubled the Nation. President Johnson steadily exerted his influence against Segregation and on behalf of Law and Order, but there was no early solution. (*)

(*) Source: (see page 124)

(1917-1993)

John Bowden Connally, Jr. was born on February 27, 1917 in Floresville, Texas, and graduated from the University of Texas School of Law. He served in the United States Navy during World War II. He was an aide to Lyndon Johnson when the latter was a young Congressman and maintained ties to Johnson while practicing Law in Texas. He was an American Politician from the State of Texas. He was a member of both the Democratic Party and the Republican Party during his life.

In 1961, President John F. Kennedy named Connally Secretary of the Navy. Connally resigned after 11 months to seek the Texas Governorship. He was elected Governor of Texas in November, 1962 as a Democrat. He served as Governor from 1963 to 1969.

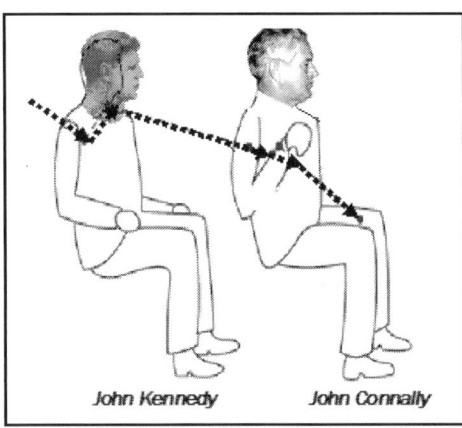

On November 22, 1963, he was seriously wounded while riding in President Kennedy's car in Dallas (see photo on your left), when the President was assassinated. He was wounded 5 times when a bullet entered through his chest, exiting below the right nipple, then entering the right wrist, shattering the radius bone, exiting, then embedding itself in his left thigh. Governor Connally was hit by the second bullet, which was 4.9 seconds before the fatal head shot to Kennedy.

President Richard Nixon appointed Connally as United States Secretary of the Treasury in 1971, he served as Secretary until 1972. In 1973, when LBJ died, Connally took part in eulogizing his old friend during burial services, along with the minister who officiated the services, Rev. Billy Graham. Later that year, he joined the Republican Party. When Vice President Spiro Agnew resigned in 1973, Connally was one of Richard Nixon's top choices for Vice President. Connally died of pulmonary fibrosis on June 15, 1993. (*)

(*) Source: (see page 124)

(1939-1963)

Lee Harvey Oswald was born on October 18, 1939 in New Orleans, Louisiana. His father, Robert Edward Lee Oswald, died before he was born, and his mother Marguerite Claverie raised him and his two older siblings, his brother Robert and his half-brother John Pic (Marguerite's child by her first marriage). His mother doted on him to excess, but despite this she was a domineering and quarrelsome woman and all three of her children entered the U.S. Armed Forces. They lived an itinerant lifestyle; before the age of 18, Oswald had lived in 22 different residences and attended 12 different Schools, mostly around New Orleans and Dallas.

Oswald (see photo on your left) was a withdrawn and temperamental child. After they moved in with John Pic, who had joined the U.S. Coast Guard and was stationed in New York City, Oswald struck and pulled a knife on his mother. His truancy caused him to be evaluated by a psychiatrist, who diagnosed the 14 year old Oswald as having a "*personality pattern disturbance with schizoid features and passive-aggressive tendencies.*" Marguerite fled back South with her son before he could be Institutionalized.

When he was enrolled in school, Oswald attended infrequently. He never received a High School diploma and was for his entire life quite a terrible speller; in fact, his letters and diary have led some to speculate that he was dyslexic. Despite this, he read voraciously and as a result thought he was better educated than those around him. Starting at around age 15, he became an ardent Communist, solely from his reading on the topic. He enlisted in the U.S. Marines 1956, a week after his seventeenth birthday. (cont.)

(Oswald cont.)

Oswald was trained as a Radar Operator and assigned to Atsugi, Japan. Though Atsugi was the Base for the U-2 Spy Planes which flew over the USSR, Oswald was not involved in that Operation. Oswald's experience in the Marine Corps was unpleasant. Small and frail compared to the other Marines, he was nicknamed "**Ozzie Rabbit**". His meekness and his Communism did not endear him to his compatriots, and the more ostracized he was, the more ardent and outspoken a Communist he became, to the point where his nickname became "**Oswaldskovich**". He subscribed to The Worker and taught himself rudimentary Russian. Oswald was Court Martial twice, first for unauthorized possession of a private weapon, and later for starting a fight with a Sergeant. As a result, he lost his promotion to Corporal and served time in the Brig. He was not punished for another incident in which he broke down and started firing his rifle into the woods. By the end of his Marine Career, he was doing menial labor.

Oswald's 1959 trip to the USSR was well planned. In addition to his studies of Russian, he saved his Marine Corps salary, he got an early discharge by claiming he needed to care for his mother (a lie), and submitted several falsified applications to Universities to aid in his quest to get a student visa. After entering the Soviet Union as part of a package tour, he declared that he wished to defect. Initially, his effort was encouraged, though as he was of little value to the USSR, his application was rejected. A despondent Oswald attempted suicide by slashing his left wrist in his hotel bathtub. With authorities fearing an international incident should Oswald attempt suicide again, Oswald was eventually allowed to stay and shipped off to Minsk, where he was kept under nearly constant surveillance during his stay in the Country.

The Minsk KGB had never had their own American case and they threw themselves into the task with gusto, the result being the lengthy KGB file no. 31451, a day by day account of Oswald's life. Initially, Oswald seemed to thrive. He had a job as a metalworker at the Belorussian Radio and Television Factory and his own rent-free apartment and monetary subsidies above his factory pay, an idyllic existence by Soviet-era working-class standards. He was called "**Alek**" by his friends, who thought "**Lee**" was too Chinese. He bought a shotgun and went hunting with friends and dated women he met at Trade Union dances. However, Oswald was tired of his life. The Bureaucracy of the Soviet Union eventually caused Oswald to believe the Country was a poorly implemented perversion of Marxist goals; he believed himself to be a pure Marxist. He grew bored with the limited recreation that Minsk offered and was stunned when a co-worker he proposed to, Ella Germann, rejected him. (cont.)

(Oswald cont.)

Lee Harvey Oswald met Marina Alexandrovna Medvedeva Nikolayevna Prusakova (see photo on your left), a 19 year old pharmacology student. They were married less than a month and a half later. It was not the ideal basis for such a union, as Oswald was on the rebound from Ella. Marina, some believe, married Oswald for his standard of living (his own apartment, etc.) or in order to immigrate to America. *"Maybe I was not in love with Alik as I ought to have been,"* she admits. This seems possible, as she later wrote love letters to two of her ex-boyfriends while in the U.S., before Oswald was accused. Marina also soon became pregnant, and gave birth to a daughter, June. Oswald renounced his renunciation of American citizenship, and after nearly a year of paperwork and waiting, the family left the USSR on June 1, 1962.

Back in the United States, the Oswald family settled in the Dallas/Fort Worth area. Oswald attempted to write a memoir and commentary on Soviet life, a small manuscript called The Collective. Oswald soon abandoned the idea, but searching for feedback did put him in touch with the area's close-knit community of Russian émigrés. They merely tolerated Oswald, but they took to Marina, feeling sorry for her because she was in a Foreign Country with no knowledge of English, which Oswald refused to teach her, and because Oswald had begun to beat her. They eventually abandoned Marina, however, because she would not leave Oswald. From this group, Oswald found an unlikely best friend, the outrageous Oil Geologist Baron George de Mohrenschildt. Perhaps they took to each other because they were polar opposites, or perhaps de Mohrenschildt, who liked playing the provocateur, enjoyed putting people off with the disagreeable and sullen Marxist Oswald. Marina also befriended a married couple, Ruth and Michael Paine.

General Edwin Walker was an anti-Communist, segregationist, and member of the John Birch Society. Walker was commanding officer of the 24th Army Division under NATO, but was relieved of this post by JFK in 1961 for distributing Right-wing literature to his troops. Walker resigned from the Army and returned to his native Texas. He ran in the six-man Democratic Gubernatorial primary in 1962 but lost to John Connally, who went on to win the race. When Walker came to Oswald's attention in February 1963, the General was making front page news by joining forces with an Evangelist in an anti-Communist Tour called *"Operation Midnight Ride"*. (cont.)

(Oswald cont.)

Oswald began to put General Walker (see photo on left) under surveillance, taking pictures of Walker's home and nearby railroad tracks, perhaps his planned escape route, using the same camera used by Marina to take the famous backyard poses. Oswald mail-ordered a rifle using his alias Hidell (he had already ordered a pistol in January). He planned the assassination on April 10, ten days after he was fired from Jaggars-Chiles-Stovall. He chose a Wednesday evening because the neighborhood would be relatively crowded because of services in a Church adjacent to Walker's home; he would not stand out and could mingle with the crowds if necessary to make his escape. He left a note in Russian for Marina with instructions should he be caught. Walker was sitting at a desk in his dining room when Oswald fired at him from less than a hundred feet (30 m) away. Walker survived only because the bullet struck the wooden frame of the window, deflecting its path, though he was injured in the forearm by fragments.

At the time, authorities had no idea who attempted to kill Walker. Marina saw Oswald burn most of his plans in the bathtub, though she hid the note he left her in a cookbook, intending to bring it to the Police should Oswald again attempt to kill Walker or anyone else. Oswald's involvement was unknown until the note and some of the photos were found by the authorities following the assassination of JFK. The bullet was too badly damaged to run conclusive ballistics tests, though neutron activation tests later proved that the bullet was from the same manufacturer as the one that killed Kennedy.

Oswald was unemployed, he had failed to kill General Walker, and his best friend, de Mohrenschildt, had moved away from Dallas. Leaving Marina (who was pregnant for the second time) with the Paines, he returned to the City of his birth to look for work, arriving on the morning of April 25. In May, Oswald got a job with the Reily Coffee Company (from which he was fired in July) and Marina joined him in New Orleans, driven there by Ruth Paine. Though Oswald got a new passport and had Marina write to the Soviet embassy about returning to the USSR, he was still disillusioned with that Country. His Marxist hopes were pinned on Fidel Castro and Cuba; he became a vocal pro-Castro advocate. (cont.)

(Oswald cont.)

The Fair Play for Cuba Committee was a National Organization and Oswald, unsolicited, set out to become a one-man New Orleans Chapter. Oswald spent $22.73 on 1000 flyers, 500 membership applications, and 300 membership cards and had Marina sign the name "A.J. Hidell" as chapter president on one of the cards. Most of Oswald's work consisted of passing out flyers. He made a clumsy attempt to infiltrate anti-Castro exile groups and briefly met with the skeptical Carlos Bringuier, the New Orleans Delegate for the Cuban Student Directorate. Several days later Bringuier and two friends confronted a man passing out pro-Castro handbills and discovered it was Oswald. In the ensuing scuffle, all were arrested and Oswald spent the night in Jail. The Trial got **Press** attention and Oswald was interviewed afterwards. He was also filmed passing out fliers in front of the International Trade Mart with two "volunteers" he had hired for $2 at the unemployment office. Oswald's work came to an end with a WDSU Radio debate between Bringuier and Oswald arranged by Journalist Bill Stuckey. Instead of discussing issues concerning Cuba, Oswald was confronted with lies and omissions he had made concerning his background. Oswald was devastated and humiliated, and a month later he left New Orleans.

Oswald's four months in the City are the subject of much attention, most notably New Orleans DA Jim Garrison's attempt to link Lee Harvey Oswald to local businessman Clay Shaw, former President of the International Trade Mart. The links between Oswald and Shaw were supposedly W. Guy Banister, a former FBI Agent turned Detective, and David Ferrie, a Pilot and amateur cancer researcher.

Ferrie and Oswald were both in the Civil Air Patrol in New Orleans in the 1950s and a CAP group photo shows them together, though there is no credible evidence that they knew each other then or in 1963. Banister had an office in the building at 544 Camp Street and Oswald stamped some (but not all) of his flyers with that address. There is also no credible evidence that Oswald knew Banister or rented an office at Banister's building, and in any case Oswald's letters, applications, etc. were constantly filled with lies. But Oswald must have known the building since the Reily Coffee Company is only a block away. It was also home to the anti-Castro Cuban Revolutionary Council, and using their address may have been Oswald's way of attempting to embarrass them. (cont.)

(Oswald cont.)

Ruth Paine (see photo on your left) drove to New Orleans to bring Marina Oswald (see photo on your left) back to Dallas, while Oswald lingered in the City for two more days in order to collect a $33 unemployment check. He boarded a bus to Houston, but instead of heading North to Dallas he boarded a bus Southwest towards Laredo and the Mexican Border. In Mexico, he planned to continue on to Cuba, a plan which he openly shared with other passengers on the bus. Once in Mexico City, he filled out a visa application at the Cuban Consulate claiming he wanted to stop there on his way back to the USSR. The Cubans insisted the USSR needed to approve his journey to that Country first before he could get a Cuban visa, and he was rejected by the Russian Consulate once they checked up on him with Moscow. After shuttling back and forth between consulates for five days, Oswald returned to Dallas. Disappointed and surprised that he was not quickly allowed into Cuba despite his work on behalf of the Cuban Revolution, he never spoke in glowing terms about Cuba or Castro again.

According to the Warren Commission Report on the John F. Kennedy assassination, Oswald shot Kennedy from a window on the sixth floor of the Texas School Book Depository, where he was employed during the Christmas rush, as the President's Motorcade passed through Dallas's Dealey Plaza at 12:30 pm on November 22nd. Texas Governor John Connally was wounded at the same time, along with an assassination witness, James Tague, who was standing some 270 feet in front of the Presidential limousine. However, critics of this account assert that photographic and filmed evidence indicate that there were at least one or two shooters in an area known as the Grassy Knoll behind a picket fence atop a small sloping hill in Dealey Plaza, to President Kennedy's right-front.

Oswald immediately headed for the back staircase, disposing of the rifle behind some boxes. On the second floor, he encountered Marion Baker, a Policeman who had driven his motorcycle to the door of the Depository and sprinted up the stairs to search for the shooter. With him was Oswald's Boss, Roy Truly, who identified Oswald as an employee, so Baker let Oswald pass. Oswald bought a Coke from a vending machine in the second floor lunchroom, crossed the floor to the front staircase, then descended and left the building through the front entrance on Elm Street. (cont.)

(Oswald cont.)

At about 12:40 pm (CST), Oswald boarded a bus by pounding on the door in the middle of the block, but when traffic slowed the bus to a halt, he requested a bus transfer from the driver. He took a cab to a point a few blocks away from his rooming house, then walked there to retrieve his pistol and beige jacket. He lingered at a bus stop across the Street then began walking. His ultimate destination is unknown, but before he was stopped, he had walked almost a mile, and was only four blocks away from a 1:40 pm bus which could have connected him with a Greyhound headed South for Mexico.

Patrolman J. D. Tippit (see upper photo) had undoubtedly heard the general description of the shooter, based on the statement Howard Brennan, who had seen Oswald in the window of the Depository from across the Street, gave to Police and was broadcast at 12:45. Tippit spotted Oswald about 1:15 pm (CST) near the corner of Patton Avenue and Tenth Street and pulled up next to him to talk to him through his car window. Tippit then got out of his car and Oswald pulled his .38 and shot him, killing him instantly. Thirteen people either witnessed the shooting or identified Oswald fleeing the scene. Oswald emptied his revolver and reloaded, leaving the shells behind. He also left his jacket in the parking lot of a nearby gas station.

He ducked into the entrance way of a shoe store on Jefferson Street to avoid some passing Police cars, then dashed into the nearby Texas Theater (see photo on your left) without paying. The shoe store's manager followed him and alerted the Ticket Clerk, who phoned Police. The Police quickly arrived and poured into the Theater, which was playing "**War Is Hell**" starring Audie Murphy. Officer M.N. McDonald saw Oswald sitting near the back and ordered him to stand. Oswald punched McDonald and drew his gun, but McDonald tackled Oswald before he could fire. Police arrested him and took him away, past a crowd who had gathered outside the Theater and shouted for Oswald's death. (cont.)

(Oswald cont.)

Oswald was arrested at the Texas Theater in the Dallas neighborhood of Oak Cliff at about 1:50 pm, first as a suspect in the shooting of Tippit and was then charged with assassinating Kennedy, even though the arraignment hearing on the Kennedy charge was abruptly interrupted and never did get finished, so he was never really officially charged with the assassination of President Kennedy. While in custody, Oswald denied the shooting, telling reporters "*I didn't shoot anyone*" and "*I'm just a patsy*". Oswald was the assassin of U.S. President John F. Kennedy on November 22, 1963, according to the conclusions of two Government investigations into the assassination. Critics of the official accounts have claimed that Oswald did not act alone or was not involved at all and was framed, but no single compelling alternative suspect has emerged.

On November 24, at 11:21 am CST
(Death of Oswald)

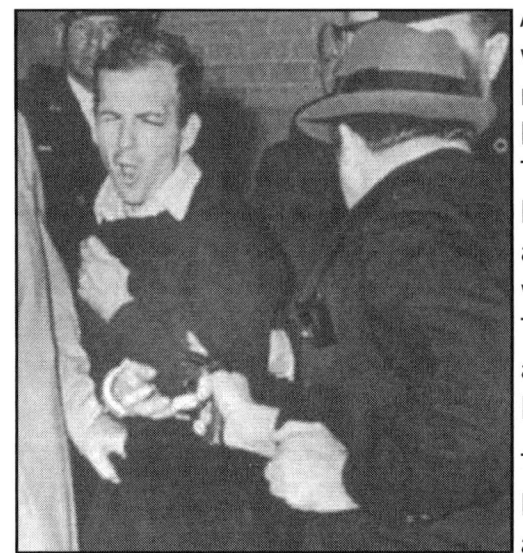

After 15 hours of undocumented interrogations, while he was being transferred via car to a nearby Jail, Oswald was shot and killed in the basement of the Dallas Police Jail, in front of live TV cameras, by Jack Ruby (see photos to your left) a Dallas Nightclub owner with friends and acquaintances in the U.S. Mafia. Millions watched the murder of Lee Harvey Oswald on Television. It was the first time in TV history that a murder was captured and shown publicly live, but it was shown live on only one network, NBC.

The route that Ruby took to get down into the basement of the Dallas Jail has been disputed, although Ruby was very specific about using the entrance ramp (and his access to the Jail on other days). This was Recorded during the polygraph test Ruby insisted on taking and documented in a Warren Report appendix. One witness, a former Policeman named Napoleon Daniels, stated that he had seen Ruby use the ramp. The use of a route through the Jail building suggests to some that Ruby had received help from authorities inside the building, however, many Journalists entered the building without having their credentials checked, and Ruby can be seen on film also inside the building on the previous Friday night, apparently posing as a Reporter. Ruby later stated that he killed Oswald on the spur of the moment to spare Jacqueline Kennedy the stress and embarrassment a Trial would cause her, (*)

(*) Source: (see page 124)

(1911-1967)

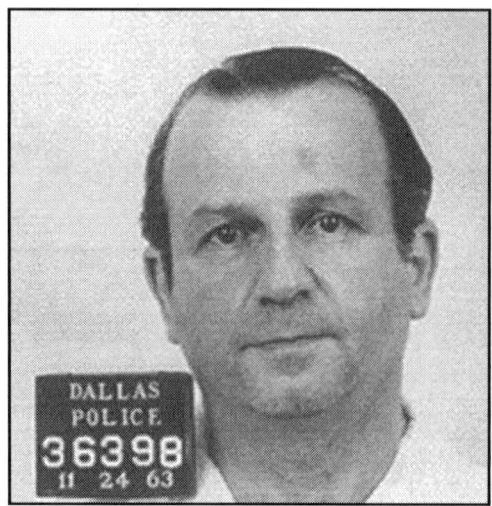

Jack Ruby was born Jacob Rubenstein to Joseph Rubenstein and Fannie Turek Rutkowski or Rokowsky in Chicago in 1911. His parents were Polish immigrants and their Religious beliefs were Orthodox Jewish. The fifth of his parents' eight living children, he had a troubled childhood and adolescence, marked by juvenile delinquency and times in foster homes. Young Ruby worked selling horse-racing tip sheets, then for a scrap-iron collectors union. He also had links to Organized Crime while working for Al Capone's Mafia Organization. He served in the United States Army during World War II without seeing combat.

In 1947, Ruby moved to Dallas, where he and his brothers soon afterward shortened their surnames from Rubenstein to Ruby. The stated reason for changing the family name had been that Jack and his brothers had opened up a mail order business and feared that some customers would refuse to do business with Jews. Jack later went on to manage various Nightclubs, strip clubs, and dancehalls. Among the strippers Ruby befriended was Candy Barr. He developed close ties to many Dallas Police Officers, who frequented his Nightclubs where Ruby showered them with large quantities of liquor and other favors. When Ruby was arrested immediately after the shooting, he told several witnesses that his killing of Oswald would show the World that "**Jews have guts**," that he helped the City of Dallas "redeem" itself in the eyes of the public, and that Oswald's death would spare Jacqueline Kennedy the ordeal of appearing at Oswald's Trial. Ruby stated that he shot Oswald to avenge Kennedy. Later, however, he claimed he shot Oswald on the spur of the moment when the opportunity presented itself, without considering any reason for doing so.

On March 14, 1964, Ruby was convicted of murder with malice, for which he received a death sentence. In June 1964, Chief Justice Earl Warren, then Representative Gerald R. Ford of Michigan, and other Commission members went to Dallas to see Ruby. Ruby asked Warren several times to take him to Washington D.C., saying "*my life is in danger here*" and that he wanted an opportunity to make additional statements. He added: "*I want to tell the truth, and I can't tell it here.*"

Ruby died of a pulmonary embolism, secondary to bronchogenic carcinoma (lung cancer), on January 3, 1967, at Parkland Hospital, where Oswald had died and where President Kennedy had been pronounced dead after his assassination. He was buried beside his parents in the Westlawn Cemetery in Norridge, Illinois. (*)

(*) Source: (see page 124)

(1924-1963)

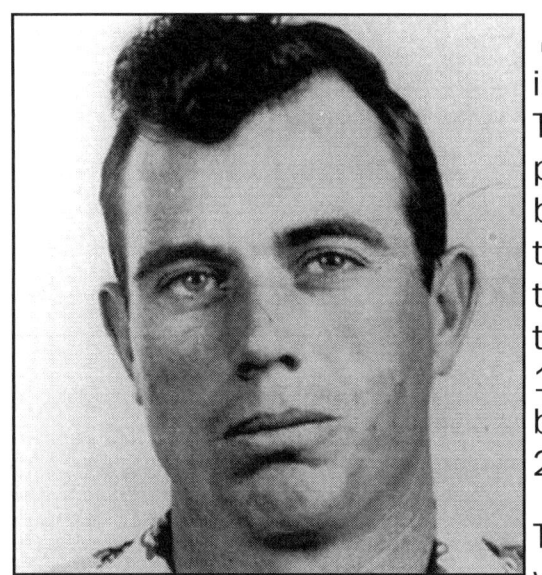

J. D. Tippit was born on September 18, 1924 in Clarksville, Red River, Texas to Edgar Lee Tippit and Lizzie Mae Rush. It is often reported that J.D. stood for "**Jefferson Davis**", but in fact, the initials do not stand for anything. Tippit attended Public Schools through the tenth grade. Tippit was a Baptist. He entered the United States Army on July 21, 1944 and was assigned to the U.S. 17th Airborne Division where he served until June 20, 1946.

Tippit was married to Marie Frances Gassaway on December 26, 1946, and they had three children. That same year, he went to work for the Dearborn Stove Company. He then worked for Sears, Roebuck and Company in the installation department from March 1948 to September of 1949, when he moved to Lone Star, Texas and attempted cattle farming.

He attended a Veterans Administration Vocational Training School at Bogata, Texas from January 1950 until June 1952. He was then hired by the Dallas Police Department as a Patrolman on July 28, 1952. He served capably and was cited for bravery in 1956 for his role in disarming a fugitive.

On November 22, 1963 Tippit volunteered to assume the watch of his friend and fellow Officer Tom Tilson. He was ordered to patrol the Oak Cliff area of Dallas after the shooting of President Kennedy. At approximately 1:15 pm, 45 minutes after the shooting, Tippit stopped Oswald, who fit the general description of the assassin. Tippit called to Oswald from the car. They spoke briefly, then Tippit got out of the car. Tippit was shot with a .38 and was killed instantly. Thirteen witnesses identified Lee Harvey Oswald as either the shooter or as fleeing the scene.

In January 1964 Tippit was posthumously awarded the Medal of Valor from the National Police Hall of Fame and also received the Police Medal of Honor, the Police Cross, and the Citizens Traffic Commission Award of Heroism. Tippit is buried at Laurel Land Memorial Park in Dallas, Texas. (*)

(*) Source: (see page 124)

(1917-1963)

John F. Kennedy was born May 29, 1917 in Brookline, Mass. President Kennedy had to deal with many serious problems here in the United States. The biggest problem of all had to do with racial discrimination. The U.S. Supreme Court had ruled in 1954 that segregation in Public Schools would no longer be permitted. Black children and White children should be able to go to School together. This was now the Law of the land.

Americans joined together, people of all races and backgrounds, to peacefully protest this injustice. Martin Luther King, Jr. was one of the famous leaders of the Movement for Civil Rights. Many Civil Rights leaders didn't think President Kennedy was supportive enough of their efforts. The President believed that holding public protests would only anger many White people and make it even more difficult to convince the members of Congress who didn't agree with him to pass Civil Rights Laws.

By June 11, 1963, however, President Kennedy decided that the time had come to take stronger action to help the Civil Rights struggle. He proposed a new Civil Rights Bill to the Congress and he went on Television asking Americans to end racism. 'One hundred years of delay have passed since President Lincoln freed the Slaves, yet their heirs, their grandsons, are not fully free,' he said. 'This Nation was founded by men of many Nations and backgrounds... [and] on the principle that all men are created equal.' President Kennedy made it clear that all Americans, regardless of their skin color, should enjoy a good and happy life in the United States.

On November 21, 1963, President Kennedy flew to Texas to give several Political speeches. The next day, as his car drove slowly past cheering crowds in Dallas, shots rang out. Kennedy was seriously wounded and died a short time later. Within a few hours of the shooting, Police arrested Lee Harvey Oswald and charged him with the murder. On November 24, another man, Jack Ruby, shot and killed Oswald, thus silencing the only person who could have offered more information about this tragic event. The Warren Commission was organized to investigate the assassination and to clarify the many questions which remained. (*)

(*) Source: (see page 124)

Chapter III

Photos of the Tragic Event in Dallas

Dealey Plaza the afternoon of November 22, 1963

Oswald's Perch, 6th floor

Grassy Knoll
Houston Street
Elm Street
Main Street

From Houston Street, the Presidential limousine made the planned left turn onto Elm Street, allowing it access to the Stemmons Freeway exit. As it turned on Elm, the motorcade passed the Texas School Book Depository. Shots were fired at President Kennedy as they continued down Elm Street. About 80% of the witnesses recalled hearing **three shots**. (*)

JFK Limousine
JFK was not Protected at all
The Grassy Knoll

(*) Source: (see page 124)

The Texas Schoolbook Depository (Where the three shots were fired from)

Oswald Sniper's Nest

2nd shot (Back)

3rd shot (Head)

1st shot (Missed)

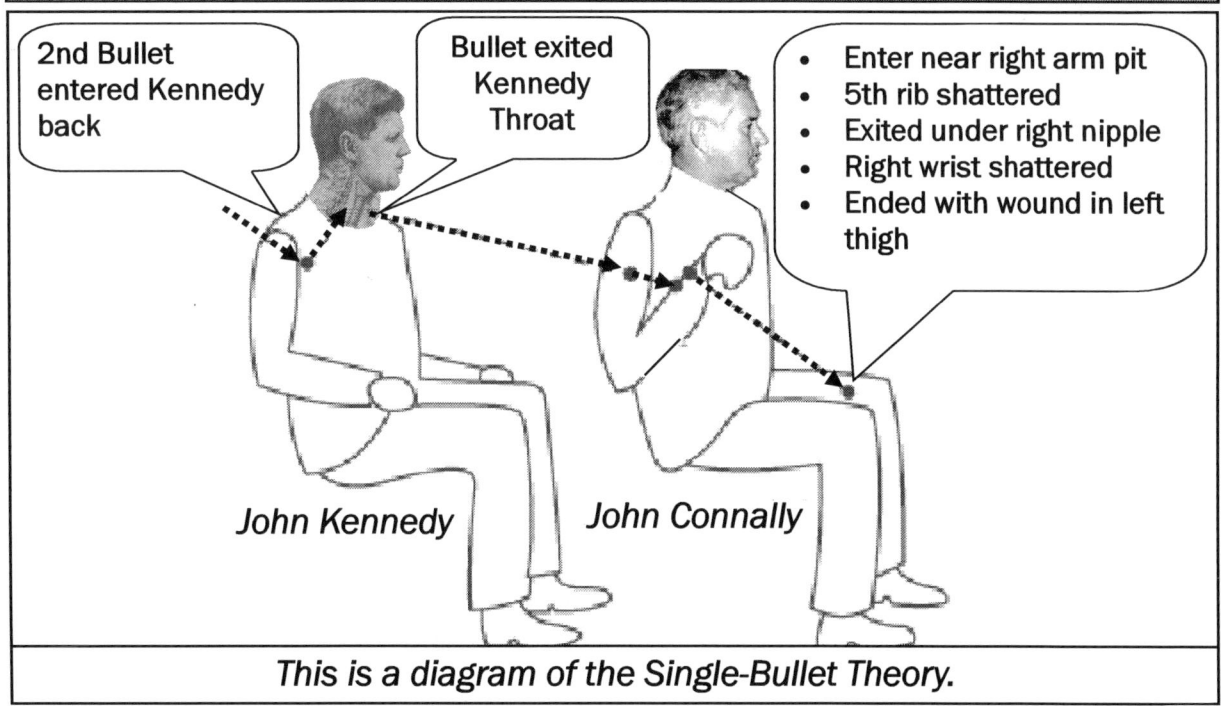

2nd Bullet entered Kennedy back

Bullet exited Kennedy Throat

- Enter near right arm pit
- 5th rib shattered
- Exited under right nipple
- Right wrist shattered
- Ended with wound in left thigh

John Kennedy   John Connally

This is a diagram of the Single-Bullet Theory.

(*) Source: (see page 124)

Texas School Book Depository Building:

Oswald's Perch

(*) Source: (see page 124)

Fifth and Sixth floors taken shortly after the assassination:

Oswald's Perch

TEXAS SCHOOL BOOK DEPOSITORY

(*) Source: (see page 124)

Arrows indicate spent shell casing on floor on November 25, 1963:

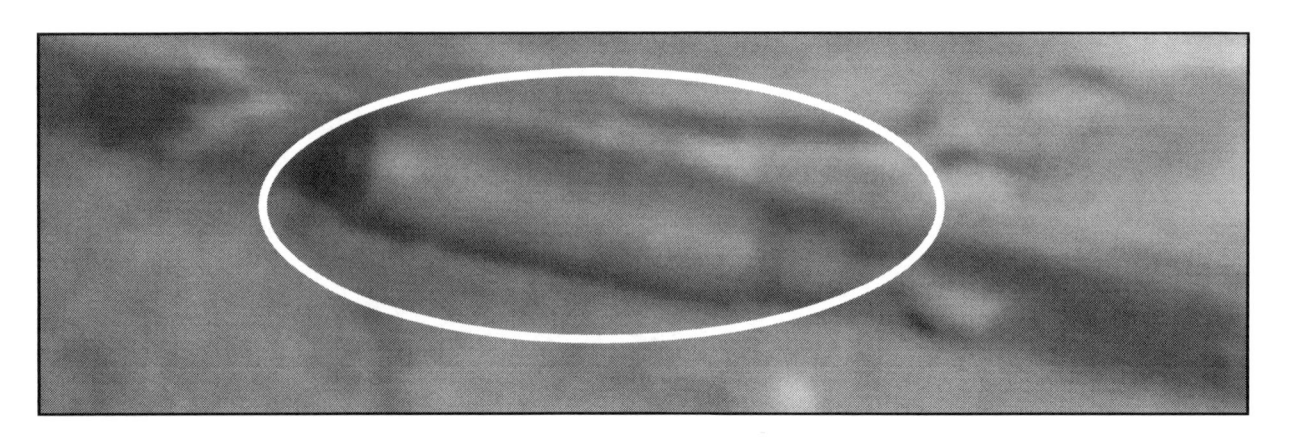

Spent shell casing on floor on November 25, 1963 (close up)

(*) Source: (see page 124)

Position of boxes in window on November 25, 1963:

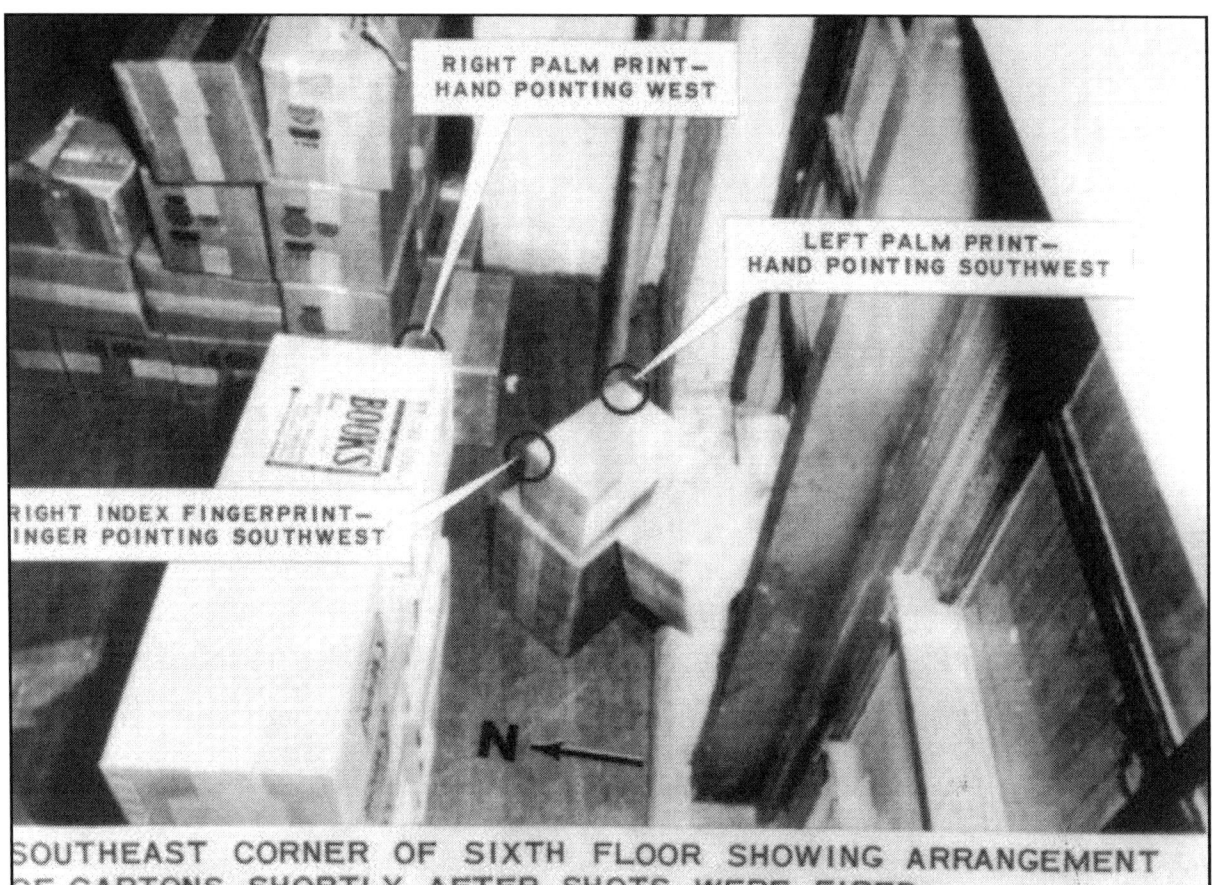

RIGHT PALM PRINT — HAND POINTING WEST

LEFT PALM PRINT — HAND POINTING SOUTHWEST

RIGHT INDEX FINGERPRINT — FINGER POINTING SOUTHWEST

SOUTHEAST CORNER OF SIXTH FLOOR SHOWING ARRANGEMENT OF CARTONS SHORTLY AFTER SHOTS WERE FIRED.

(*) Source: (see page 124)

Position of boxes in window and rifle he used, on November 25, 1963:

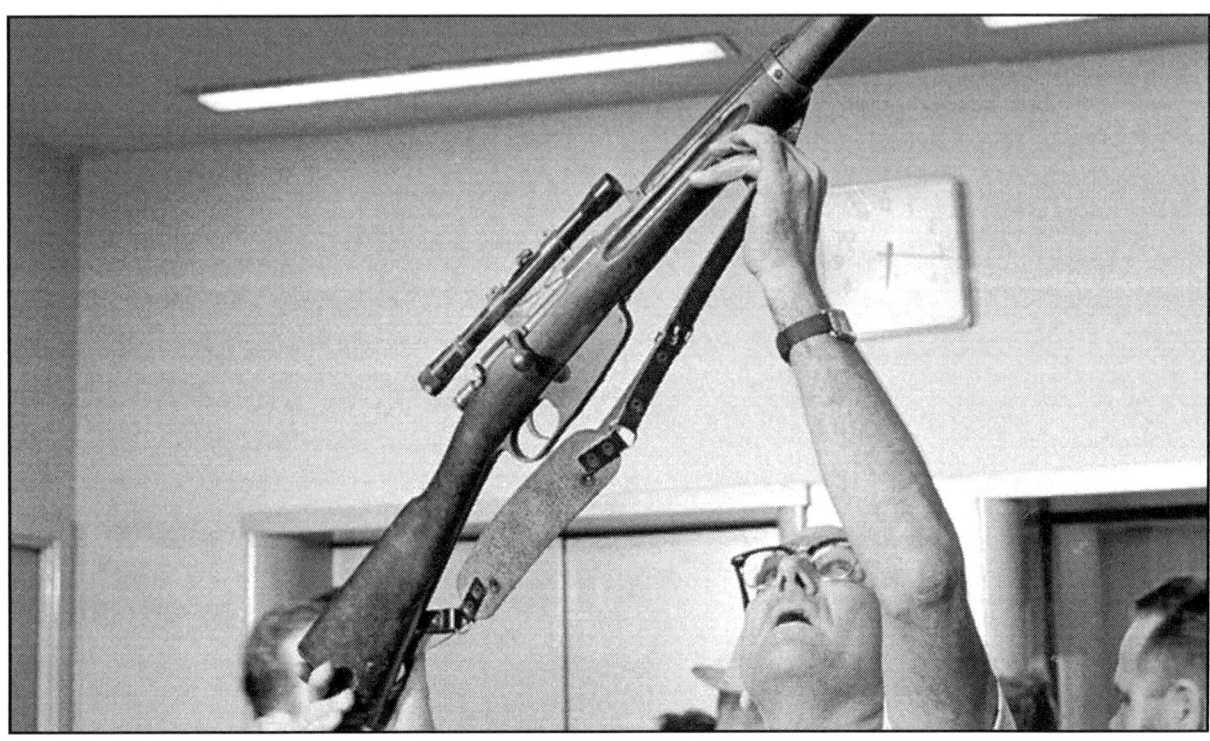

(*) Source: (see page 124)

Oswald's mug shot and finger prints:

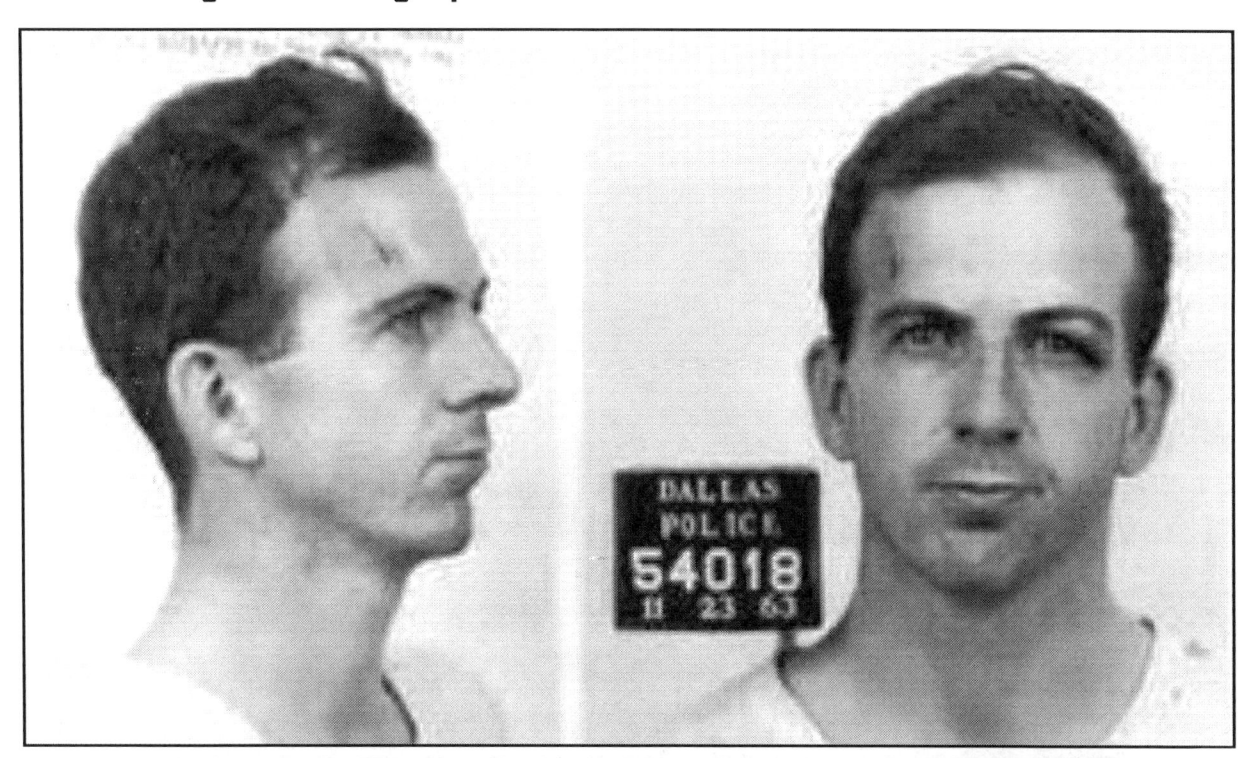

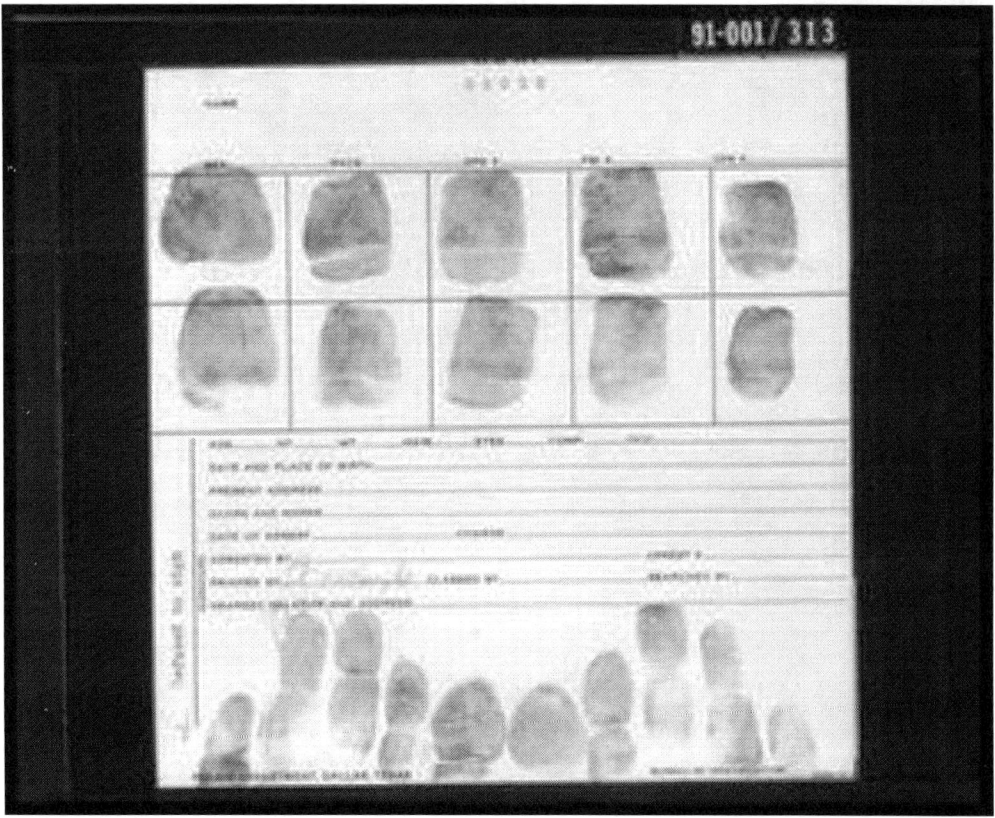

(*) Source: (see page 124)

Oswald bought rifle into the Depository concealed in a long paper bag:

(*) Source: (see page 124)

Oswald's arrest and death:

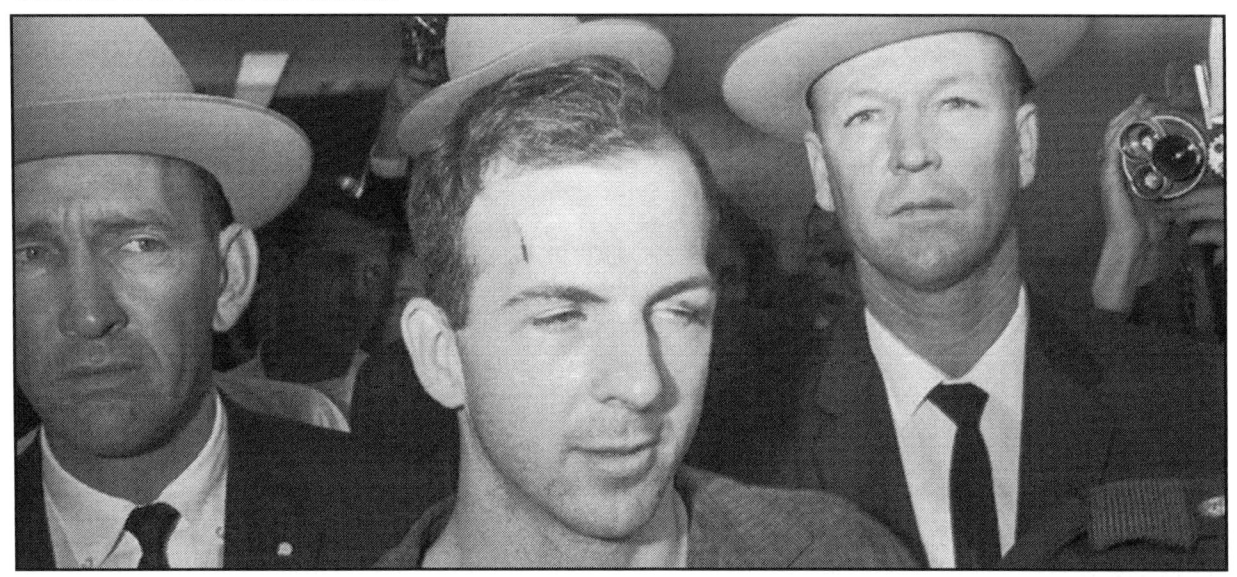

(*) Source: (see page 124)

The boarding house where Oswald rented and his room:

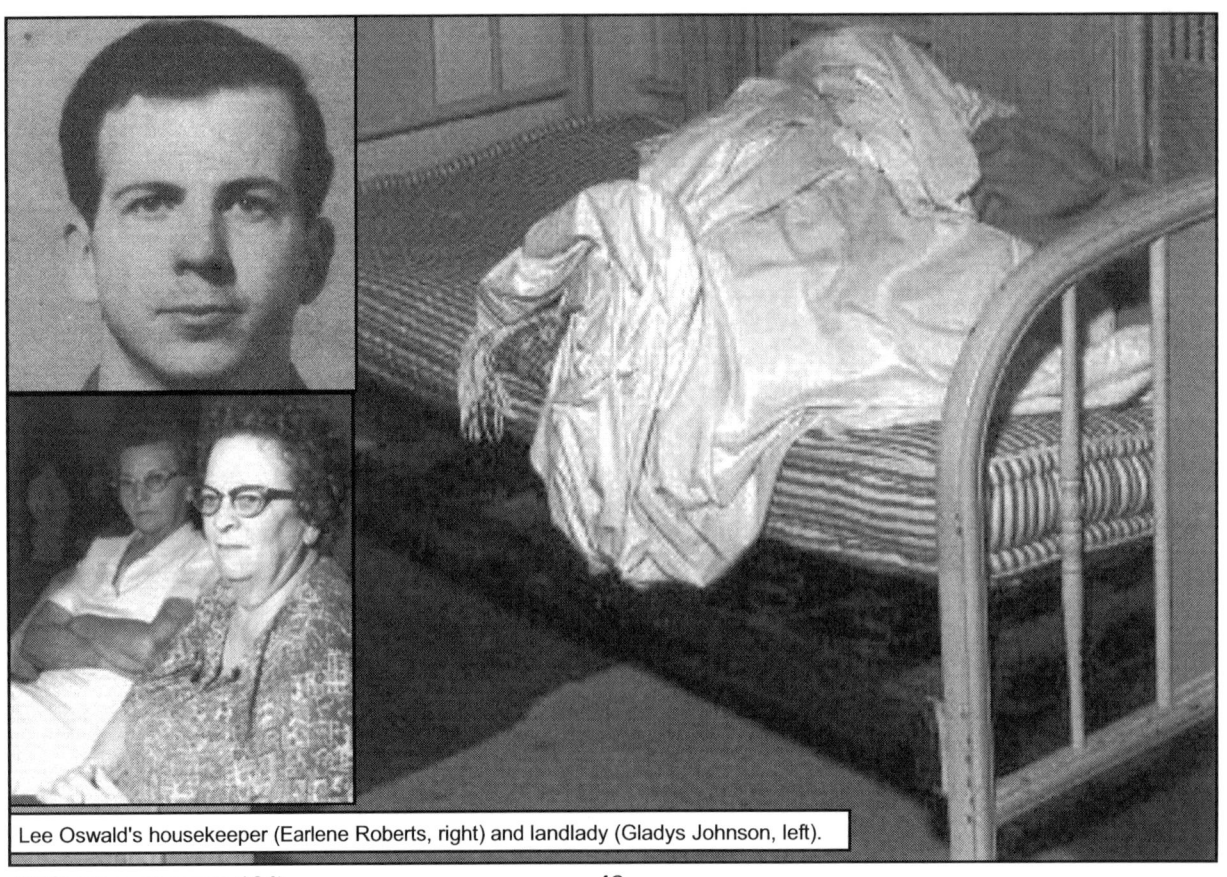

Lee Oswald's housekeeper (Earlene Roberts, right) and landlady (Gladys Johnson, left).

(*) Source: (see page 124)

Chapter IV

Dealey Plaza Witnesses

(Witness No. 1)

Abraham Zapruder took the most famous piece of amateur motion picture film in history. At the time of the assassination, Zapruder was an admirer of President Kennedy and considered himself a Democrat. Zapruder had originally planned to film the motorcade carrying President Kennedy through downtown Dallas on November 22, but decided not to film the event as it had been raining that morning. When he arrived at work that morning without his camera, Zapruder's assistant insisted that he retrieve it from home before going to Dealey Plaza because the weather had cleared.

Zapruder agreed to give the film to Sorrels on the condition it would be used only for investigation of the assassination. The three then took the film to the television station WFAA to be developed. After it was realized that WFAA was unable to develop Zapruder's footage, film was taken to Eastman Kodak's Dallas processing plant where it was immediately developed later that afternoon.

As the Kodachrome process requires different equipment for duplication than for simple development, Zapruder's film was not developed until around 6:30 p.m. The original developed film was taken to the Jamieson Film Company, where three additional copies were exposed; these were returned to Kodak around 8 pm. for processing. Zapruder kept the original, plus one copy, and gave the other two copies to Sorrels, who sent them to Secret Service headquarters in Washington.

Zapruder added that he had assumed the shots came from behind him because the President's head went backwards from the fatal shot, and also that the wound on the side of the President's head was facing that direction. He also said he believed it because Police Officers ran to the area behind him. He broke down and wept as he recalled the assassination, and did so again at the 1969 Trial of Clay Shaw. Zapruder died of stomach cancer in Dallas on August 30, 1970, and is buried in the Emanu-El Cemetery in Dallas. (*)

(*) Source: (see page 124)

(Witness No. 2)

Roger Craig is the guy featured in lots of conspiracy books. You remember: he saw Oswald run from the School Book Depository and get in a Rambler on Elm Street, supposedly belonging to Mrs. Paine, a few minutes after the assassination. Immediately after this Craig was told by Sheriff Decker to help the police search the TSBD. Deputy Craig was one of the two people to find the three rifle cartridges on the floor beneath the window on the Southeast corner of the sixth floor. He saw lots of other suspicious stuff too. Was it really a Rambler? Was it really Mrs. Paine's? Did a photo really show up years later to vindicate Craig? Check out this detailed analysis of his testimony.

(Witness No. 3)

Seymour Weitzman, the Officer who first saw Oswald's rifle behind some boxes on the 6th floor of the Texas School Book Depository, said it was a Mauser, and several other officers repeated this statement. Before the Warren Commission, Weitzman said that "in a glance" the gun looked like a Mauser. This photo, taken from *Six Seconds in Dallas*, shows Oswald's Mannlicher-Carcano beside a Mauser. So you be the Judge: could someone "in a glance" mistake one rifle for the other? (Warning: this is a very large image. You may wish to download and print, rather than view it.)

- Regardless of what any witness said, WFAA-TV cameraman Tom Alyea was on the sixth floor of the Depository photographing the recovery of the rifle. Here is one frame from his 16 mm. film, and here is another. The rifle in the film is not merely a Mannlicher-Carcano, a distinctive mark on the gun identifies it as Oswald's Mannlicher-Carcano. The same gun in the backyard photos, and the same gun that sits to this day in the National Archives. (*)

(*) Source: (see page 124)

(Witness No. 4)

Marilyn Sitzman. Among the Dealey Plaza witnesses, Marilyn Sitzman was superbly positioned to see what was going on. Standing on the same pedestal with Abraham Zapruder (and helping steady him), she was only a few yards from the supposed position of the Grassy Knoll shooter. She saw Kennedy hit in the head, and she turned to look in the direction of the Stockade Fence after the head shot. Although she did not testify before the Warren Commission, author Josiah Thompson interviewed her. Here is a transcript of that interview.

(Witness No. 5)

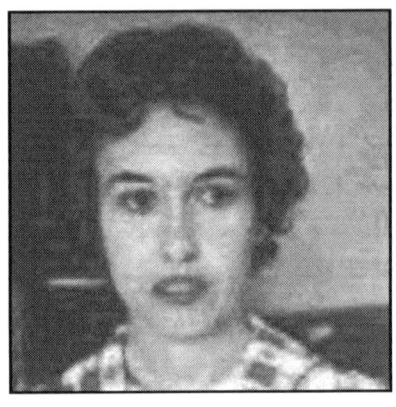

Julia Ann Mercer. Mercer, you may remember, told the story of seeing Jack Ruby at the wheel of a pickup truck near the Triple Underpass just a couple of hours before the assassination. She claimed another man took a gun case from the back of the pickup and walked up a grassy incline toward the Grassy Knoll. What really happened?

- First, the transcript from the Dallas Police Department radio log, describing the broken-down pickup truck that was the basis of Mercer's tale.
- Then the account of Secret Service agent Forest Sorrels, to whom Mercer told an early version of her story.
- Mercer's deposition given to the Dallas County Sheriff's Department on November 22, 1963.
- Mercer's statements to the FBI in the week following the assassination.
- Statements from Dallas Police Department officers who witnessed the breakdown of the pickup truck on November 22nd, 1963.
- Mercer's story as recounted in Jim Garrison's book, A Heritage of Stone.
- Mercer's story as told to conspiracy author Henry Hurt. You'll note one extremely interesting addition to the story here.

The question, as with all assassination witnesses is: is she credible? (cont.)

(Witness No. 6)

Jean Hill is the woman in the red raincoat, plainly visible in the movies and still photos of Dealey Plaza. She has always had interesting stories to tell, from seeing a little dog in the limo between Jack and Jackie Kennedy, to her current claim to have seen a Grassy Knoll shooter in the act of shooting. How consistent has her testimony been? How does it accord with other evidence?

(Witness No. 7)

Tom Tilson tells of seeing a man scrambling down the bank behind the Grassy Knoll on the West side of the Triple Underpass immediately following the assassination, putting an object (a rifle?) in a car, and driving off. Might this be the Grassy Knoll shooter? Or might Tom Tilson be telling tall tales? Peter Whitney examines the credibility of Tilson in this article, reprinted from Back Channels.

(Witness No. 8)

Phil Willis. You can see Phil Willis in the conspiracy videos claiming that the back of Kennedy's head was blown out. He even puts his hand on the back of his head to show where he supposedly saw Kennedy's head explode. His Warren Commission testimony is a bit different.

(Witness No. 9)

Jackie Kennedy is widely quoted in assassination books as a witness who claimed to have seen a wound on the back of Kennedy's head. Here is her account of the terror of Dealey Plaza, as told to Theodore White. It provides an interesting supplement to her Warren Commission testimony.

(Witness No. 10)

Rufus Youngblood, Secret Service Agent Rufus W. Youngblood was in Dealey Plaza at the time of the assassination, protecting Vice President Johnson. In 1992 Gary Goettling, a writer for the *alumni magazine* of Georgia Tech, interviewed him. The assassination related portions of the resulting article, *"Eyewitness to the Death of a President"*, are now available. (cont.)

(Witness No. 11)

Texas Monthly Witnesses:

- On the 35th Anniversary of the assassination, the "*Texas Monthly*" interviewed several key witnesses, and published the unedited transcripts on their web site. The witnesses are Bill and Gayle Newman, Pierce Allman, Bobby Hargis, Rosemary Willis Roach, James Leavelle, Waggoner Carr, Nellie Connally, and Red Duke. Interesting material indeed, although 35 year old testimony can't be as reliable as contemporaneous testimony.

(Witness No. 12)

Ed Hoffman, Ed Hoffman is a deaf mute who was on the Stemmon Freeway onramp at the time of the shooting. He now claims to have seen two men behind the Stockade Fence, one firing a shot at Kennedy and another disassembling the gun. FBI documents from the 1960s don't show him mentioning any shooter. Is this an FBI "**cover-up**," miscommunication, or yet another witness who has changed his story? See Ed Hoffman: Did He See a Grassy Knoll Shooter?

"Dealey Plaza Witnesses" Who weren't in the Plaza?

- Many Dealey Plaza films and photos show a figure dubbed "the Babushka Lady" standing on the South Side of Elm, filming the assassination with what appears to be a movie camera. Just how credible is Oliver? (*)

(*) Source: (see page 124)

(Witness No. 14)

Gordon Arnold was born on August 14, 1941 in Dallas, Texas. He is a man who claimed to be a witness to the John F. Kennedy assassination. Arnold served three years in the United States Army, after enlisting in 1963. After being discharged from the Army, he married (one living son as of 2004) and Arnold became employed with the Dallas Department of Consumer Affairs in Dallas, Texas.

In 1978 Arnold first publicly claimed to have been a witness to the 1963 assassination of John F. Kennedy in Dealey Plaza in Dallas. He claimed that minutes before the assassination he was twice approached by a business suited CIA or Secret Service Agent who demanded he move away from behind the picket fence of the Dealey Plaza north Grassy Knoll. He claimed he moved just South of the picket fence and then filmed the assassination with a movie camera from a few feet north of a 3.3' high cement retaining wall on the Grassy Knoll, and that a bullet passed extremely close to his left ear, then he dove to the ground. Arnold said that very soon after the end of the attack a man armed with a revolver and dressed in a Dallas Police uniform kicked him while Arnold was still laying on the ground then demanded his movie film while another man armed with a rifle and also dressed in a Dallas Police uniform and wearing yellow lens tinted "shooter's glasses" stood close by crying, shaking, and waving his rifle around. Arnold claimed he gave the revolver armed Policeman his movie camera, the policeman removed the film, then returned the camera to Arnold (now with the Policeman's fresh fingerprints).

Three days later Arnold said he reported for his pre-assassination-scheduled transfer to the U.S. Army's Fort Wainwright in Alaska. Despite his claims being made public some five months before the House Select Committee on Assassinations investigation ended, the HSCA, which did learn of his claims, decided not to interview him. After 1978 Arnold provided his claims to only a few assassination researchers and book authors. Some persons claim that Arnold has not been found in any of the photographs or films of the assassination. No witnesses ever reported seeing him, including Abraham Zapruder and his assistant standing very near where Arnold claimed to be, but who were focused on watching the President. Some researchers claim to have photographically enhanced his U.S. Army uniformed image in a Polaroid photograph taken by Mary Moorman during the assassination, while others claim this is actually the theorized "badge Man" or simply just a tree or shadow. Gordon died on October 15, 1997. (*)

(*) Source: (see page 124)

(Witness No. 15)

Lee Bowers was a witness to the assassination of John F. Kennedy in 1963. He reported seeing people standing on the Grassy Knoll, and said that something (he was not sure what) drew his eye toward that area at the time of the shooting.

Lee Bowers testimony is perhaps as explosive as any recorded by the Warren Commission. He was one of the 65 witnesses who saw the President's assassination, and who thought shots were fired from the area of the Grassy Knoll. (The Knoll is West of the Texas School Book Depository Building.) But more than that, he was in a unique position to observe some pretty strange behavior in the Knoll area before and during the assassination. Bowers, then a Tower man for the Union Terminal Co., was stationed in his 14 foot Tower directly behind the Grassy Knoll. He faced the scene of the assassination. He could see the railroad overpass to his right. Directly in front of him was a parking lot and a wooden stockade fence, and a row of trees running along the top of the Grassy Knoll. The Knoll sloped down to the spot on Elm Street where the President was killed. Police had "cut off" traffic into the parking lot, Bowers said, "*so that anyone moving around could actually be observed.*"

Bowers made two significant observations which he revealed to the Warren Commission. First, he saw three unfamiliar cars slowly cruising around the parking area in the 35 minutes before the assassination; the first two left after a few minutes. The driver of the second car appeared to be talking into a "*mike or telephone*"; "*he was holding something up to his mouth with one hand and he was driving with the other.*" A third car with out-of-state license plates and mud up to the windows, probed all around the parking area. Bowers last remembered seeing it about eight minutes before the shooting, pausing "*just above the assassination site.*"

Bowers also observed two unfamiliar men standing on the top of the Knoll at the edge of the parking lot, within 10 or 15 feet of each other. "One man, middle aged or slightly older, fairly heavy set, in a white shirt, fairly dark trousers. Another man, younger, about mid-twenties, in either a plaid shirt or plaid coat or jacket." Both were facing toward Elm and Houston in anticipation of the Motorcade. The two were the only strangers he remembered seeing. His description shows a remarkable similarity to Julia Ann Mercer's description of two unidentified men climbing the Knoll. (cont.)

(Bowers cont.)

"The darker dressed man was too hard to distinguish from the trees." Bowers observed *"some commotion"* at that spot . . .," " . . . *something out of the ordinary, a sort of milling around . . . which attracted my eye for some reason which I could not identify."* At that moment, a motorcycle Policeman left the Presidential motorcade and roared up the Grassy Knoll, straight to where the two mysterious gentlemen were standing. Later, Bowers testified that the *"commotion"* that caught his eye may have been a *"flash of light or smoke."*

BEFORE ME, Patsy Collins, a Notary Public in and for said County, State of Texas, on this day November 23, 1963 Lee E. Bowers, Jr., w/m/38 of 10508 Maple grove Lane, Dallas, Texas DA-1-1909 who, after being by me duly sworn, on oath deposes and says:

> I work at North Tower Union Terminal Co. RI-8-4698 7 am to 3 pm Monday thru Friday. The tower where I work is West and a little North of the Texas Book Depository Building. I was on duty today and about 11:55 am I saw a dirty 1959 Oldsmobile Station Wagon come down the street toward my building. This Street dead ends in the railroad yard. This car had out of State license plats with white background and black numbers, no letters. It also had a Goldwater for "64" sticker in the rear window. This car just drove around slowly and left the area. It was occupied by a middle aged White man partly grey hair. At about 12:15 pm another car came into the area with a White man about 25 to 35 years old driving. This car was a 1957 Ford, black, 2 door with Texas license. This man appeared to have a mike or telephone in the car. Just a few minutes after this car left at 12:20 pm another car pulled in. This car was a 1961 Chevrolet, Impala, 4 door, I am not sure that this was a 4 door, color white and dirty up to the windows. This car also had a Goldwater for "64" sticker. This car was driven by a White male about 25 to 35 years old with long blond hair. He stayed in the area longer than the others. This car also had the XXX [strikeout] same type license plates as the 1959 Oldsmobile. He left this area about 12:25 pm. About 8 or 10 minutes after he left I heard at least 3 shots very close together. Just after the shots the area became crowded with people coming from Elm Street and the slope just North of Elm.
> Lee E. Bowers Jr.

On the morning of August 9, 1966, Lee Powers, Vice President of a construction firm, was driving South of Dallas on business. He was two miles South of Midlothian, Texas when his brand new company car veered from the road and hit a bridge abutment. A farmer who saw it, said the car was going about 50 miles an hour, a slow speed for that road. Bowers died in a Dallas hospital. He was 41. There was no autopsy and he was cremated. A Doctor from Midlothian who rode to Dallas in the ambulance with Bowers, noticed something peculiar about the victim. *"He was in some strange sort of shock."* The Doctor said, *"A different kind of shock than an accident victim experiences. I can't explain it. I've never seen anything like it."* When I questioned his widow, she insisted there was nothing suspicious, but then became flustered and said, *"They told him not to talk."* (*)

(*) Source: (see page 124)

(Witness No. 16)

Charles F. Brehm was a witness to the assassination of President John F. Kennedy within Dealey Plaza in Dallas Texas on November 22, 1963. Charles F. Brehm and his 5-year-old son Joe were standing in the Dealey Plaza north infield grass, a few feet south of the south curb of Elm Street, across the street from Abraham Zapruder and the Dealey Plaza grassy knoll. They can both be clearly seen in the Zapruder film. Brehm was a World War II Veteran who served in the United States Army Rangers and fought on D-Day. He later fought in the Korean War.

When the Presidential limousine turned from Main Street onto Houston Street Brehm and his son watched from that intersections Northwest side. After watching the turn, Brehm and his son quickly ran Northwestward across the "*North infield grass*" towards the south curb of Elm Street to catch another glimpse of the President. They were standing close to the South curb directly across the Street from Bill and Gayle Newman and their two boys, about 20' Northeast from close assassination witnesses Jean Hill, and Mary Moorman as the limousine rounded the 120-degree slow turn from Houston Street onto Elm Street. The movie filming "***Babushka lady***" was standing nearby to Brehm's right backside.

Brehm said President Kennedy was approaching him and only 30' away when his son then started to wave to President Kennedy, and the President started to wave back, then Brehm heard the first shot he remembered hearing. President Kennedy did not start waving until Zapruder film frame Z-173, which was after live oak tree branches and foliage had already temporarily hidden the President from Z-162 to Z-208 from being seen by anyone in the Texas School Book Depository's sixth-floor window, the location of assassin Lee Harvey Oswald. Brehm stated to the FBI that "*he could see the President's face very well, the President was seated, but was leaning forward when he stiffened perceptibly*" and "*seemed to stiffen and come to a pause*" when the first shot Brehm remembered hearing was also the first shot that impacted the President and the President reacted immediately to being impacted. When the President was 15' to 25' away, and had just passed, Brehm remembered hearing a second shot that struck President Kennedy in the head. (cont.)

(Brehm cont.)

Brehm watched the President's "*hair fly up*," "*ripple*," and "*bits of brain and bone went flying*" and "*then roll over to his side*" then President Kennedy "*slumped all the way down.*" The location of Brehm's November 22, 1963 written Dallas police voluntary affidavit statement is unknown. In the 1966 video documentary Rush to Judgment while speaking of the blood cloud and the bits of brain and bone matter that Brehm saw flying in the air when the President's head exploded, Brehm stated he was specifically attracted to watch a piece fly towards himself, "*over in the area of the curb where I was standing.*" ... "*It seemed to have come left, and back.*" ... "*Sir, whatever it was that I saw did fall, both, in that direction, and, over into the curb there.*"

Charles Brehm was behind and to the President's left when the President's head first exploded. On November 22, 1963 while still standing within Dealey Plaza, and only minutes after the assassination, Brehm was quoted by a Reporter as saying that Brehm, "*seemed to think the shots came from in front of, or, beside the President.*" In his November 24, 1963 FBI statement and during the 1987 Showtime cable-TV mock Trial, The Trial of Lee Harvey Oswald, Brehm testified that the shots came from either the Texas School Book Depository or the Dal-Tex building.

In 1988, Brehm told author Larry Sneed, "*After the car passed the building coming toward us, I heard a . . . surprising noise, and (the President) reached with both hands up to the side of his throat and kind of stiffened out . . . And when he got down in the area just past me, the second shot hit which damaged, considerably damaged, the top of his head. . . . That car took off in an evasive motion . . . and was just beyond me when a third shot went off. The third shot really frightened me! It had a completely different sound to it because it had really passed me as anybody knows who has been in down under targets in the Army or been shot at like I had been many times. You know when a bullet passes over you, the cracking sound it makes, and that bullet had an absolute crack to it. I do believe that that (third) shot was wild. It didn't hit anybody. I don't think it could have hit anybody. But it was a frightening thing to me because here was one shot that hit him, obviously; here was another shot that destroyed his head, and what was the reason for that third shot? That third shot frightened me more than the other two, and I grabbed the boy and threw him on the ground because I didn't know if we were going to have a 'shoot-'em-up' in this area.*"

Just like many other supporting witnesses, Brehm stated he remembered hearing another shot after the President's head had already exploded. Charles Brehm was not called to testify publicly in front of the Warren Commission, but he did supply a deposition. Brehm died on August 8, 1996. (*)

(*) Source: (see page 124)

(Witness No. 17)

James M. Chaney was born on March 8, 1921 was a witness and Dallas Police motorcycle Presidential escort riding only ten to fifteen feet away from (slightly behind and to the right of) President John F. Kennedy during his assassination on November 22, 1963 within Dealey Plaza in Dallas, Texas. In a November 22, 1963 interview with Reporter Bill Lord Recorded by Dallas ABC TV, Chaney stated he remembered hearing three shots. Chaney said when he heard the first shot he remembered that it sounded like a motorcycle backfiring and Chaney immediately looked to his left and saw President Kennedy had "*looked back over his left shoulder*" within the limousine. In the famous Ike Altgens photo taken concurrent with Zapruder film frame 255, Chaney is seen very close to the limousine facing President Kennedy. Chaney further stated that "*the second shot hit him in the face*," and that a third shot was fired that Chaney did not see hit the President but he did see Governor John B. Connally's shirt erupt in blood. Chaney stated that the shots he remembered hearing seemed to come from "*back over my right shoulder*." During the assassination his police uniform was spattered with blood and President Kennedy's head matter.

On November 23, 1963 Chaney was stationed on duty within Dealey Plaza and spoke with Nightclub owner and alleged organized crime member Jack Ruby when Ruby stopped by the Plaza to see the memorial wreaths, flowers, and messages placed there by mourners. James Chaney, the closest non-limousine witness to the President during the assassination, was never called by the Warren Commission to testify. Chaney died a relatively young man in April, 1976 from a heart attack.

The Warren Commission's 75-year rule no longer exists, supplanted by the **Freedom of Information Act** of 1966 and the **JFK Records Act** of 1992. By 1992, 98 percent of the Warren Commission Records had been released to the public. Six years later, at the conclusion of the Assassination Records Review Board's work, all Warren Commission Records, except those Records that contained tax return information, were available to the public with only minor redactions. The remaining Kennedy assassination related documents are scheduled to be released to the public by 2017, twenty-five years after the passage of the **JFK Records Act.** (*)

(*) Source: (see page 124)

(Witness No. 18)

William Greer was born in County Tyrone, Ireland, in 1910. His family emigrated to the United States. Greer worked as a farm laborer before moving to Boston where he became a chauffeur. After the bombing of Pearl Harbor Greer joined the U.S. Navy. He was assigned to the Presidential Yacht in May 1944. At the end of the Second World War Greer joined the U.S. Secret Service. He joined the staff of the White House in November, 1950. Over the next thirteen years he worked as a chauffeur for Harry S. Truman, Dwight Eisenhower, and John F. Kennedy.

On the 22nd November, 1963, Greer was assigned to drive the Presidential car in the motorcade through Dallas. Several witnesses said that Greer stopped the car after the first shot was fired. This included Jean Hill, who was the closest witness to the car when Kennedy was hot: According to Hill "*the motorcade came to almost a halt at the time the shots rang out*". James Chaney (one of the four Presidential motorcyclists) - stated that the limousine "*after the shooting, from the time the first shot rang out, the car stopped completely, pulled to the left and stopped.*" Mary Woodward, a journalist with the **Dallas Morning News** wrote: "*Instead of speeding up the car, the car came to a halt... after the first shot*".

In Greer's defense, it must be said that his seatmate, Agent Roy Kellerman, was the senior agent. Secret Service procedures in place at the time did not allow Greer to take action without orders from Kellerman. Between the second and third shots, however, the latter claims he shouted, "*Let's get out of line, we've been hit,*" but that Greer apparently turned to look at Kennedy (for the second time), long enough for Kennedy to receive the fatal head shot, before accelerating the car out of the danger zone. As Roy Kellerman told author William Manchester, "*Greer then looked in the back of the car. Maybe he didn't believe me.*" Since that time, Secret Service agents have been trained to accelerate rapidly out of the area if they even think they hear gunfire.

Like all of the agents on duty during the assassination, Greer was neither reprimanded nor disciplined for his role. He retired on disability from the Secret Service in 1966, citing a stomach ulcer that allegedly grew worse following the Kennedy assassination. In 1973 he relocated to Waynesville, North Carolina, where he died of Cancer on February 23, 1985. (*)

(*) Source: (see page 124)

(Witness No. 19)

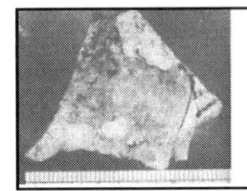

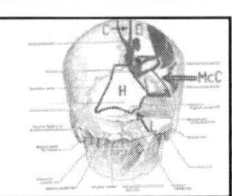

William "Billy" Allen Harper - On November 22, 1963 he was a Texas Christian University medical student who after the assassination of President John F. Kennedy, Harper discovered a large piece of President Kennedy's skull bone (referred to as the "Harper fragment") in the grass to the left and forward of President Kennedy, South of Elm Street.

After discovering the "**Harper fragment**" on 11-23-63 at 5:30 pm CST, Harper gave the skull piece to his uncle, Jack C. Harper, a medical Doctor at the "Methodist Hospital" of Dallas. The same day Jack gave the skull piece to A. B. Cairns, a medical Doctor and Chief Pathologist of "Methodist Hospital." On 11-25-63 Cairns gave the skull piece to FBI Special Agent James W. Anderton, who notified his FBI superiors in Washington D.C., who ordered that the skull fragment be sent for examination at the FBI laboratory in D.C..

Harper has diagramed where he found the skull piece. The found location was 117' forward of the President's Z-313 head explosion location, to the left side of the limousine, but, to the right side of President Kennedy's facing direction.

A theorized straight-line flight path of the "Harper fragment," back through the President's Street point location at Z-313, continues behind the President and intersects the West side of the sixth-floor Depository windows -not the Warren Commission Eastern-most snipers lair- where, just minutes before the assassination a Warren Commission witness, Arnold Rowland, testified that he observed a second rifle-armed assassin standing with the weapon held at a military-like "port arms" position through a sixth floor West window.

(just minutes after the assassination, Rowland voluntarily approached a Dallas Police Detective and volunteered that he had seen a second rifle armed man in the sixth floor west window). By 1:15 pm CST Rowland also told Secret Service Agent in charge of the Motorcade, Forrest Sorrels that he had seen two armed men on the sixth floor of the Depository. William Harper was never called by the Warren Commission to testify. (*)

(*) Source: (see page 124)

(Witness No. 20)

Jean Lollis Hill was born on February 11, 1931 in Oklahoma. She was a witness to the John F. Kennedy assassination. She was known as the **'Lady in Red'** because of the long red rain coat she wore that day, and was captured in the Zapruder Film. She was portrayed in the film JFK by Ellen McElduff. She was present along with her friend Mary Moorman across from the Grassy Knoll, and was one the very closest witnesses to President John F. Kennedy when the shots were fired at him.

In Jean Hill's Warren Commission documented testimony she stated that an "Agent" told her 11-22-63 right after the attack that another "Agent," watching from the Court House, saw a bullet strike, "*at my feet*" and kick up debris. (There were not, officially, any "Agents" ever documented to have been stationed within the Dealey Plaza grounds or surrounding buildings during the assassination.)

At Z-313, when President Kennedy's head exploded, Jean Hill was only 21' away, leftward, and slightly behind President Kennedy. Hill was also one of several witnesses who have stated that at the end of the assassination she saw smoke lingering near the Grassy Knoll picket fence corner. She also testified to the Warren Commission that after the assassination she was attracted to watch a man running from near the Depository towards the picket fence area. After watching this man, Hill crossed the Street and ran with many other witnesses and authorities who first ran towards the Grassy Knoll after the shots ended.

During her commission testimony she stated that as the limousine came abreast of her she saw what she thought was a small white dog in between President Kennedy and his wife. As is documented in films and photos captured at Love Field, Mrs. Kennedy was also given a small bouquet of white flowers that she held together with a bouquet of red roses, and had laid upon the limousine seat during the Motorcade. Many of her claims have not held up to scrutiny. She claimed Jack Ruby was in Dealey Plaza when witnesses placed him in the offices of the **Dallas Morning News**. She claims she immediately crossed the Street and ran up the Grassy Knoll when pictures taken of the scene show her sitting and standing in her original position. To the Warren Commission and in a Television interview an hour after the assassination, she said she did not see the shots, but after 1978 claimed to have seen a shooter on the Grassy Knoll. She died on November 7, 2000. (*)

(*) Source: (see page 124)

(Witness No. 21)

Roy Kellerman was born on March 14, 1915 in Macomb County, Michigan native, graduated from High School in 1933, and worked for the Dodge Division of Chrysler sporadically from 1935 until 1937 when he was sworn in as a Trooper for the Michigan State Police. Kellerman joined the Secret Service in Detroit just before Christmas, 1941, transferring temporarily to the White House detail in March 1942 and permanently one month later. As the Secret Service Agent, Assistant in Charge of November 22, 1963 Shift Team #3, Kellerman was riding in the front passenger seat of the Presidential limousine.

Kellerman was the nearest agent to the President during the attack, and testified to the Warren Commission that after he remembered hearing his first audible muzzle blast or mechanically-suppress-fired bullet bow shockwave, that the assassination then ended in a "flurry of shells" coming into the limousine that reminded him of a jet sonic-boom sound quickness.

Kellerman also testified to the Warren Commission, "*I am going to say that I have, from the firecracker report and the two other shots that I know, those were three shots. But, Mr. Specter, if President Kennedy had from all reports four wounds, Governor Connally three, there have got to be more than three shots, gentlemen.*" Kellerman further testified to the Warren Commission, "*I turned around to find out what happened when two additional shots rang out and the President slumped into Mrs. Kennedy's lap and Governor Connally fell to Mrs. Connally's lap.*"

Like all of the agents on duty during the assassination, Kellerman was neither reprimanded nor disciplined for his role. Indeed, he was promoted, retiring from the Secret Service in 1968 as an assistant administrator. He died in St. Petersburg, Florida on March 22, 1984.

Kellerman's widow, June, told author Vince Palamara on March 2, 1992 that her husband believed there was a conspiracy involved in the death of JFK (Of course, the existence of a conspiracy would tend to lessen Kellerman's own responsibility.) (*)

(*) Source: (see page 124)

On Sept. 26, 1963, the two Dallas newspapers confirmed plans of the Nov. visit.

There were concerns about security, because as recently as October 24, 1963, United States Ambassador to the United Nations, Adlai Stevenson, had been jeered, jostled, struck by a protest sign and spat upon during a visit to Dallas. The danger from a concealed sniper on the Dallas trip was also of concern. President Kennedy himself had mentioned it the morning he was assassinated, as had the Secret Service agents when they were fixing the Motorcade Route.

Sgt. Davis, of the Dallas Police Department, had prepared the most stringent security precautions in the City's history, so that the demonstrations like those marking the Stevenson visit would not happen again. But Winston Lawson of the Secret Service, who was in charge of the planning, told the Dallas Police not to assign its usual squad of experienced homicide detectives to follow immediately behind the President's car. This Police protection was routine for both visiting Presidents and for Motorcades of other visiting dignitaries. Police Chief Jesse Curry later testified that had his men been in place, the murder might have been prevented, because they carried submachine guns and rifles to take out any attackers, or at least they might have been able to stop Oswald before he left the building.

It was planned that Kennedy would travel from Love Field Airport in a Motorcade through Downtown Dallas (including Dealey Plaza) to give a speech at the Dallas Trade Mart. The car in which he was traveling was a 1961 Lincoln Continental, open-top, modified limousine. No presidential car with a bullet-proof top was yet in service in 1963, though plans for such a top were presented in October 1963.

> *"I, Myself would have been leery of my security with their lax attitude of protecting the President. The ones that should be protection the President could have been setting him up for a target. I have always ponder the thought of the President riding in a convertible in a hostile City like Dallas with it tall buildings. My first thought would insist the President ride in a limo with a top if I had to protect him.*
>
> *"Nevertheless, Kennedy probably felt something strange were going to happen and he went on with the plan to visit Dallas anyway. Furthermore most Whites in the South were furious about Kennedy integration policy. By killing Kennedy and making him a martyr did nothing but speed up changes in this country for the betterment of all citizens. Maybe that was the price President Kennedy had to pay to change status quo. This is my personal opinion."*
>
> *Therlee Gipson*

Different signs to welcome President John F. Kennedy:

(*) Source: (see page 124)

Chapter V

Who Really Killed JFK?

17 Theories on Who Killed JFK

Theory No. 1: Lee Harvey Oswald and the CIA.

Theory No. 2: The Mafia.

Theory No. 3: The Soviet Union.

Theory No. 4: Right-Wing Activists in New Orleans.

Theory No. 5: Antoine Guerini and the Marseilles Mafia.

Theory No. 6: Lyndon B. Johnson and Texas Oil Millionaires.

Theory No. 7: David Atlee Phillips and the CIA.

Theory No. 8: Rogue Members of the CIA.

Theory No. 9: Jack Ruby and the Mafia.

Theory No. 10: E. Howard Hunt and the CIA.

Theory No. 11: The Mafia, Anti-Castro Activists and the CIA.

Theory No. 12: CIA and Executive Action.

Theory No. 13: Secret Service Conspiracy.

Theory No. 14: J. Edgar Hoover and the FBI.

Theory No. 15: John Birch Society.

Theory No 16: The Three Tramps .

Theory No 17: Anti Integration Group.

NOTE: Several factions of the CIA had plots against the President. (cont.)

Where Did the Term "Grassy Knoll" Come From?

35 ear witnesses who were present at the shooting thought that shots were fired from in front of the President — from the area of the "Grassy Knoll" (see photo on your left) or Triple Underpass — while 56 ear witnesses thought the shots came from the Depository, or at least in that direction, behind the President, and 5 ear witnesses thought that the shots came from two directions.

The Umbrella Man:

Was this fellow, standing in Dealey Plaza with an open umbrella and no rain in sight part of some conspiracy? The House Select Committee on Assassinations located the Umbrella Man -- a fellow named Louis Witt who was engaged in a somewhat obscure form of political protest. Here are two graphics, one showing Louis Witt's umbrella being opened before the House Select Committee on Assassinations, to the general merriment of all assembled. The second shows the Umbrella Man's umbrella in the Zapruder film in Dealey Plaza. Both of these images are video captures from the NOVA documentary. Here is the first one, and here is the second. Some conspirator finalists claim that the umbrellas are different, having a different number of spokes. Decide for yourself.

- What was the point of the umbrella in Dealey Plaza? Apparently it was an attempt to heckle Kennedy with a reminder of the appeasement policies of British Prime Minister Nevill Chamberlain, whose weak posture toward Hitler was supported by Kennedy's father. Sounds pretty obscure to us today. But this 1930s British cartoon links the umbrella (Chamberlain's trademark) with weakness toward Nazism.

- One of the more bizarre theories about The Umbrella man comes from Robert Cutler. Cutler claimed that the umbrella was a weapon firing a flechette (poisoned dart) that hit Kennedy in the throat, paralyzing Kennedy to set him up for the head shot. (*)

(*) Source: (see page 124)

Theory No. 1: Lee Harvey Oswald

Lee Harvey Oswald (see photo on left). Was involved in a conspiracy to assassinate the President not known to this day. This theory has been supported by several other investigators including Arlen Specter, Walter Cronkite, Dan Rather, Hugh Aynesworth, Gerald Posner, John McAdams and Kenneth A. Rahn.

However, The Warren Commission came to the conclusion that John F. Kennedy was assassinated by a lone gunman,

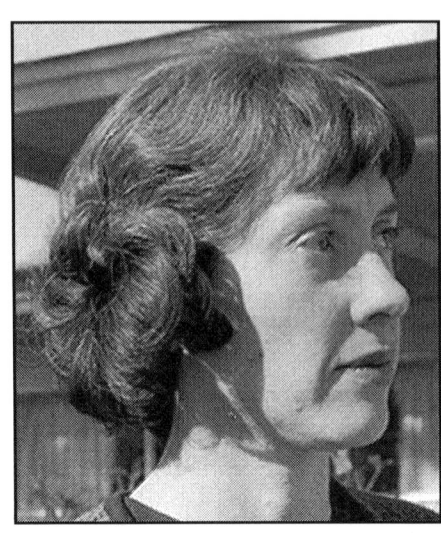

Ruth Paine (see photo on left) met the Oswalds through her interest in Russian. Oswald stored the 6.5 mm caliber Carcano rifle that he used to assassinate President John F. Kennedy in Ruth Paine's garage,

Ruth Paine drove Marina Oswald to New Orleans when the Oswalds moved there in May 1963 and back to Dallas when they moved again in September 1963. When the Oswalds resettled in the Dallas area, Marina and Lee's child, June, moved in with Ruth Paine

At the suggestion of a neighbor, Ruth Paine told Lee Oswald about a job opportunity at the Texas School Book Depository, where he was hired oddly quick. Lee Harvey Oswald stayed at the Paine home with Marina and his children unannounced on Thursday night, November 21, 1963—the night before President Kennedy was assassinated.

When Oswald left for work on the morning of November 22, he brought a large package that he had kept in the Paine's garage with him to work at the Texas School Book Depository. Oswald's coworker and friend, Wesley Frazier testified that Oswald told him the bag contained curtain rods. The evidence demonstrated that the package actually contained the rifle used by Oswald in the assassination. (*)

(*) Source: (see page 124)

Theory No. 1: Lee Harvey Oswald (cont.)

Harold Norman (see photo on left) moved to Dallas in 1961 and later that year found work at the Texas School Book Depository as an order filler. A fellow worker was Lee Harvey Oswald but he later told the Warren Commission Lee Harvey Oswald came over to him and asked, *"What's everybody looking at, and what's everybody excited about?"* Norman replied:

"So I told him we was waiting on the President. So he just snudged up and walked away." He later told the Warren Commission: *"I can't remember what the exact time was but I know I heard a shot, and then after I heard the shot, well, it seems as though the President, you know, slumped or something, and then another shot... I know I heard a third shot fired, and I could also hear something sounded like the shell hulls hitting the floor and the ejecting of the rifle, it sounded as though it was to me."* Norman also claimed he was convinced that the shots had "came from up above us."

Roger Craig (see photo on left) was a Deputy Sheriff in Dallas at the time of the assassination of President Kennedy. Immediately after the incident, Craig was told by Sheriff Decker to help the Police search the TSBD. Deputy Craig was one of the two people to find the three rifle cartridges on the floor beneath the window on the Southeast corner of the sixth floor. All three were no more than an inch apart and all were lined up in the same direction. One of the three shells was crimped on the end which would have held the slug. It had not been stepped on but merely crimped over on one small portion of the rim. The rest of that end was perfectly round.

After Craig went back down to Elm Street, He saw a light green Rambler station wagon coming slowly West on Elm Street, pull over to the North curb and pick up the man coming down the hill. By this time the traffic was too heavy for him to be able to reach them before the car drove away going West on Elm. (*)

(*) Source: (see page 124)

Theory No. 2: The Mafia

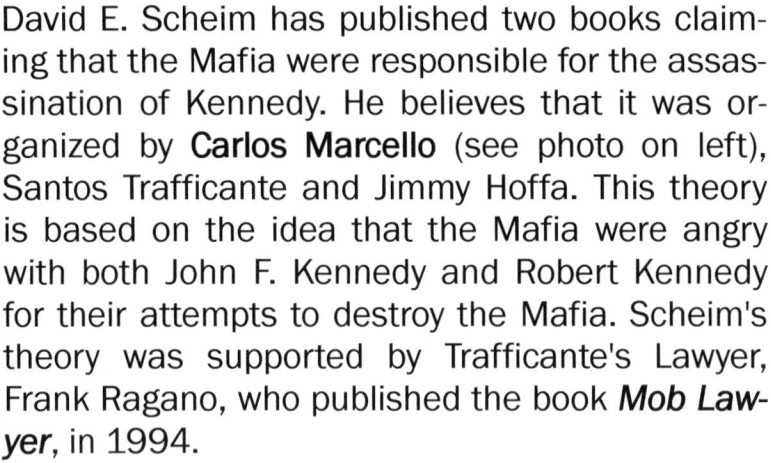

David E. Scheim has published two books claiming that the Mafia were responsible for the assassination of Kennedy. He believes that it was organized by **Carlos Marcello** (see photo on left), Santos Trafficante and Jimmy Hoffa. This theory is based on the idea that the Mafia were angry with both John F. Kennedy and Robert Kennedy for their attempts to destroy the Mafia. Scheim's theory was supported by Trafficante's Lawyer, Frank Ragano, who published the book **Mob Lawyer**, in 1994.

The theory is also supported by the investigative journalist, Jack Anderson. G. Robert Blakey, Chief Counsel and Staff Director to the House Select Committee on Assassinations from 1977 to 1979, published *The Plot to Kill the President* in 1981. In the book Blakey argues that Lee Harvey Oswald was involved but believes that there was at least one gunman firing from the Grassy Knoll. Blakey came to the conclusion that the Mafia Boss, Carlos Marcello, organized the assassination.

Undercover informants reported that Marcello made several threats against John F. Kennedy, at one time uttering the traditional Sicilian death threat curse, *"Take the stone from my shoe"*. Some of those who knew him, however, suggested that Marcello did not know enough Italian to utter such a threat. In September 1962, Marcello told private investigator Edwin Nicholas Becker that, *"A dog will continue to bite you if you cut off its tail...,"* (meaning Attorney General Robert Kennedy.), *"...whereas if you cut off the dog's head."* (meaning President Kennedy), *"... it would cease to cause trouble"*. Becker reported that Marcello, *"clearly stated that he was going to arrange to have President Kennedy killed in some way"*. Marcello told another informant that he would need to take out *"insurance"* for the assassination by, *".... setting up some Nut to take the fall for the job, just like they do in Sicily"*. (*)

(*) Source: (see page 124)

Theory No. 3: The Soviet Union

James Angleton believed that **Nikita Khrushchev** (see photo on your left) sought revenge after he had been humiliated by Kennedy during the Cuban Missile Crisis. In his book, ***Khrushchev Killed Kennedy*** (1975), Michael Eddowes argued that Kennedy was killed by a Soviet Agent impersonating Lee Harvey Oswald. ***In Legend: The Secret World of Lee Harvey Oswald*** (1978), Edward Jay Epstein argues that Oswald was a KGB Agent.

Theory No. 4: Right-Wing Activists in New Orleans

Jim Garrison, the District Attorney of New Orleans, believed that a group of Right-wing Activists, including Guy Bannister, David Ferrie, Carlos Bringuier and Clay Shaw were involved in a conspiracy with the Central Intelligence Agency (CIA) to kill Kennedy.

Garrison's key witness against Clay Shaw was Perry Russo, a 25-year-old insurance salesman from Baton Rouge, Louisiana. At the Trial, Russo testified that he had attended a Party at anti-Castro activist David Ferrie's apartment.

At the Party, Russo said that Lee Harvey Oswald (who Russo said was introduced to him as "Leon Oswald"), David Ferrie, and "Clem Bertrand" (who Russo identified in the Courtroom as **Clay Shaw** (see bottom photo)) had discussed killing President Kennedy. The conversation included plans for the **"triangulation of crossfire"** and alibis for the participants.(*)

(*) Source: (see page 124)

Theory No. 5: Antoine Guerini and the Marseilles Mafia.

Stephen Rivele (see photo on left) argued in the 1988 Television Documentary, *The Men Who Killed Kennedy* that the Kennedy's assassination had been organized by Antoine Guerini, the Corsican Crime Boss in Marseilles. He also claimed that Lucien Sarti had been one of the gunmen. In return for Rivele's help, David told him that Kennedy's assassination had been organized by Antoine Guerini, the Corsican Crime Boss in Marseilles.

David turned down the contract but was accepted by Lucien Sarti and two other members of the Marseilles mob. According to David, Sarti fired from behind the wooden fence on the Grassy Knoll. The first shot was fired from behind and hit Kennedy in the back. The second shot was fired from behind, and hit John Connally. The third shot was fired from in front, and hit Kennedy in the head. The fourth shot was from behind and missed. (*)

Theory No. 6: Lyndon B. Johnson and Texas Oil Millionaires.

Madeleine Brown claims that she was Johnson's mistress. In her autobiography, *Texas in the Morning* (1997) Brown claims that the conspiracy to kill Kennedy involved **Lyndon B. Johnson** (see photo on you left) and several Texas oil men including Clint Murchison, Haroldson L. Hunt and J. Edgar Hoover. Joachim Joesten, an investigative Journalist, believes that Johnson's Secretary, Bobby Baker was involved in this plot. This theory was supported by Craig Zirbel in his book *The Texas Connection: The Assassination of President John F. Kennedy* (1991). (*)

(*) Source: (see page 124)

Theory No. 7: David Atlee Phillips and the CIA

Gaeton Fonzi (see photo on left) was a Staff investigator for the House Select Committee on Assassinations. In his book, *The Last Investigation*, Fonzi takes the view that the assassination was organized by David Atlee Phillips (see bottom photo), head of the CIA's Western Hemisphere Division.

Fonzi was shocked at Specter's hesitant responses in particular regarding the location of the wound in Kennedy's back, concluding with Specter saying "*I don't really remember...*" In August 1966, Fonzi published an article in Philadelphia concluding "*It is difficult to believe the Warren Commission report is the truth*". (*)

Theory No. 8: Rogue Members of the CIA

David Atlee Phillips (see photo on left), head of the CIA's Western Hemisphere Division, told Kevin Walsh, a former investigator with the House Select Committee on Assassinations: that Kennedy had been "*done in by a conspiracy, likely including rogue American intelligence people.*" Unlike the Federal Bureau of Investigation (FBI), which is a domestic security service, CIA has no Law enforcement function and is mainly focused on overseas intelligence gathering, with only limited domestic collection.

Though it is not the only U.S. Government Agency specializing in HUMINT, CIA serves as the National manager for coordination and deconfliction of HUMINT activities across the entire Intelligence Community (*)

(*) Source: (see page 124)

Theory No. 9: Jack Ruby and the Mafia

The Journalist, Dorothy Kilgallen, believed that the assassination of Kennedy had involved **Jack Ruby** (see photo on your left) and the Mafia. She also suggested that J. D. Tippet and Bernard Weismann were involved in the conspiracy.

Many researchers contend Ruby was involved with major figures in organized crime, and conspiracy theorists widely assert that Ruby killed Oswald as part of an overall plot surrounding the assassination of President Kennedy. Others have argued against this, saying that Ruby's connection with gangsters was minimal at most, or circumstantial, and also that Ruby was not the sort to be entrusted with such an act within a high-level conspiracy. (*)

Theory No. 10: E. Howard Hunt and the CIA

In his book, *Plausible Denial* (1991), Mark Lane argues that CIA Agents killed Kennedy. He claims that the conspiracy involved **E. Howard Hunt** (see photo on left) and Frank Sturgis.

The Rockefeller Commission reported in 1975 that they investigated the allegation that Hunt and Sturgis, on behalf of the CIA, participated in the assassination of Kennedy. The final report of that commission stated that witnesses who testified that the "*derelicts*" bore a resemblance to Hunt or Sturgis "*were not shown to have any qualification in photo identification beyond that possessed by an average layman*". According to the Committee, only Chrisman resembled any of the tramps but determined that he was not to be in Dealey Plaza on the day of the assassination. (*)

(*) Source: (see page 124)

Theory No. 11: The Mafia, Anti-Castro Activists and the CIA

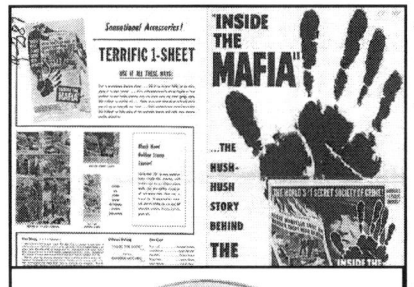

Anthony Summers is the author of *The Kennedy Conspiracy*. He believes that Kennedy was killed by a group of anti-Castro activists, funded by Mafia mobsters that had been ousted from Cuba. Summers believes that some members of the CIA took part in this conspiracy.

Summers speculated that the following people were involved in this conspiracy: Johnny Roselli, Carlos Marcello, Santos Trafficante, Sam Giancana, David Ferrie, Gerry Patrick Hemming, Guy Bannister and E. Howard Hunt.

Hunt was undeniably bitter about what he perceived as President John F. Kennedy's lack of commitment in overturning the Fidel Castro regime. In his semi-fictional autobiography, *Give Us This Day*, he wrote: *"The Kennedy administration yielded Castro all the excuse he needed to gain a tighter grip on the Island of Jose Marti, then moved shamefacedly into the shadows and hoped the Cuban issue would simply melt away."* (*)

Theory No. 12: CIA and Executive Action

Executive Action, was a CIA secret plan to remove unfriendly Foreign leaders from power. In his book *The Secret Team* (1973) **Leroy Fletcher Prouty** (see photo on left) claimed that elements of the CIA were worked on behalf of the interests of a "high cabal" of industrialists and bankers.

He also claimed that the Executive Action unit could have been used to kill Kennedy. Prouty named CIA operative, Edward Lansdale, as the leader of the operation. (*)

(*) Source: (see page 124)

Theory No. 13: Secret Service Conspiracy.

In his book, *Best Evidence*, David Lifton claims that members of the Secret Service Agents were involved in the killing of Kennedy. This included providing the assassins with a good opportunity to kill Kennedy. Lifton was highly critical of the behavior of William Greer, Roy Kellerman and Winston G. Lawson during the assassination. Lifton believes that after the assassination of Kennedy they hijacked the body in order to alter the corpse. In the book, Mortal Error, Bonar Menninger, claims that SS Agent George Hickey killed Kennedy by accident.

Theory No. 14: J. Edgar Hoover and the FBI.

J. Edgar Hoover (see photo on left) was concerned that Kennedy would force him into retirement when he reached the age of 70. Mark North (Act of Treason) and George O'Toole (The Assassination Tapes) both believe that Hoover either knew of plans to kill Kennedy and did nothing to stop them, or he helped to organize the assassination. In his book, *Deep Politics and the Death of JFK* (1993) Peter Dale Scott provides information that Hoover and the Federal Bureau of Investigation helped to cover-up the real identity of the people who assassinated John F. Kennedy.

Late in life and after his death, Hoover became a controversial figure as evidence of his secretive abuses of power began to surface. He was found to have exceeded the jurisdiction of the FBI and to have used the FBI to harass Political dissenters and activists, to amass secret files on Political leaders and to collect evidence using illegal methods. Hoover consequently amassed a great deal of power and was in a position to intimidate and threaten sitting Presidents. However, Richard Nixon was recorded as stating in 1971 that one of the reasons why he did not fire Hoover was that he was afraid of reprisals against him from Hoover. (*)

(*) Source: (see page 124)

Theory No. 15: John Birch Society:

Harry Dean (see photo on left) was an undercover Agent for the Federal Bureau of Investigation. In 1962 he infiltrated the John Birch Society. He later reported that the Society hired two gunman, Eladio del Valle and Loran Hall, to kill President John F. Kennedy.

Theory No 16: The Three Tramps:

The three hobos (see photo on left) arrested in a train yard near Dealey Plaza in the wake of the assassination. But if you have a very active imagination, and if you are quite convinced that there must have been sinister goings-on in and around Dealey Plaza, the tramps can look very suspicious indeed.

The tramps were clearly under arrest. They were taken to the Sheriff's office and questioned. But the arrest records — if there were any arrest records — had disappeared. Nobody knew whether they existed, or where they were. Nobody could find them. The notion that three tramps arrested shortly after the assassination in the train yards adjacent to Dealey Plaza were sinister conspirators.

But it's also been one of the most popular conspiracy theories, enshrined in dozens of conspiracy books. Thus by the late 1970s, conspiracist "researchers" had identified at least five of the three. The first tramp in line was thought to be Thomas Vallee, or Frank Sturgis (of Watergate fame) or Daniel Carswell. The second tramp in line was identified as either Sturgis or Carswell. The last tramp was "identified" as E. Howard Hunt or Fred Chrisman. (*)

(*) Source: (see page 124)

Theory No 17: Anti Integration Group (KKK)

"Kennedy was appointing more Blacks to Federal Government posts. He appointed 40 to Senior Federal Government positions including five as Federal Judges. He appointed Robert Kennedy as head of the Justice Department which would eventually bring 57 Lawsuits against local Officials for obstructing the African-American's Right to Vote. But in many ways, Kennedy created many enemies while trying to change the status quo." (*)

Day after Kennedy assassination:

(*) Source: (see page 124)

Chapter VI

A New View of Old Evidence

A New View of Old Evidence:

- Martin Shackleford thought it would be interesting to have a couple of professional lip readers carefully scrutinize the Zapruder film. The essay that resulted, "Listening to the Zapruder Film," seems rather modest and insignificant when read in isolation. In conjunction with careful study of the contradictory testimony of John and Nellie Connally, and of the Zapruder film, it puts a key piece of the puzzle in place. This first appeared in the March 1987 issue of The Third Decade.

- Another "new view" of the Zapruder film is made possible of a new video version, made from high-resolution scans and including the area between the sprocket holes. Now, the Zapruder film is history's greatest Rorschach test. People see all kinds of things in it, many of them downright wacky. But careful study really does yield insights about the assassination, as this essay by Steve Barber shows.

- The history of the Zapruder film, as well as a discussion of what it shows about John Kennedy's wounds and reactions, can be found in this essay by Jerry Organ.

What Can We Learn from the Damage to the Limo?

- In "Best Witness: JFK's Limousine" researcher Tony Marsh works on the premise that witness testimony is unreliable, but that the damage to the presidential limo is the sort of hard physical evidence that can be relied upon. See what a detailed look at the damage to the presidential limousine shows about the shooting.

Grassy Knoll Shooter: Blowing Smoke.

Conspiracy authors seldom fail to discuss several witnesses who saw "smoke," or "steam," or "motorcycle exhaust" on the Grassy Knoll Of course, they forget the "steam" and "motorcycle exhaust" and present all the witnesses as having seen smoke from a rifle. But just how much smoke do modern rifles produce? One clue comes from the movie "*JFK*." Director Oliver Stone could not find a rifle that would emit the necessary cloud of smoke when fired, and so he resorted to having a special-effects man blow smoke from a bellows. Many consider this an appropriate metaphor for the entire movie. (*)

(*) Source: (see page 124)

The Smell of "Gunpowder" in the Plaza.

- Conspiracy authors also mention several witnesses who said they smelled gunpowder in Dealey Plaza in the wake of the shooting. This is claimed to prove a Grassy Knoll shooter, since supposedly smoke from the Sniper's Nest could not have drifted down into the Plaza. But one witness who was a hundred yards upwind of the Plaza smelled "gunpowder." Either the smell of shots can travel further than we assume, or (more likely) witnesses didn't smell gunpowder at all.

New Film Evidence?

- Recent media attention has been focused on a film shot in Dealey Plaza, at the time of the assassination, by Patsy Paschal. Does the film show evidence of a shooter on the Grassy Knoll? Dallas researcher Greg Jaynes, in this essay, gives a thorough rundown of the film's content.

A Secret Service Man on the Knoll?

- Officer Joe Marshall Smith, who was on the Grassy Knoll behind the Stockade Fence after the shooting, was convinced that he encountered a Secret Service agent. But the Secret Service claimed to have no agents in Dealey Plaza immediately after the shooting. Was this a conspirator assigned to protect the escape of a shooter? Researcher Chris Mills suggests a different possibility in this essay.

- The standard conspiracy position -- that the "Secret Service man" was a conspirator -- is expressed in this essay by Michael T. Griffith. Written in response to Mills essay (above), it's on the JFK Lancer web site.

- A less conspiratorial view of Officer Smith's encounter with the "Secret Service man" is given by the House Select Committee, and by author Gerald Posner. There was, it seems, plenty of room for simple mistaken identity. (*)

(*) Source: (see page 124)

Acoustic Evidence of Four Shots?

That's what the House Select Committee on Assassinations claimed, based on impulses on a Dallas Police Dictabelt tape. Supposedly, one set of "impulses" showed a shot from the Grassy Knoll.

But this supposedly "scientific" evidence of conspiracy didn't survive the scrutiny of the best scientists, who gathered under the auspices of the National Academy of Sciences, and declared the acoustic analysis to be bad science. And it also didn't survive the scrutiny of an amateur but highly perceptive researcher named Steve Barber, who discovered something about the Dictabelt that the House Committee's high-priced consultants had not noticed. It's a story about the misuse of science, and of the taxpayers' money.

The Limo Slowed When the Shooting Started:

Conspiracy-oriented author Vince Palamara provides an extensive list of sources that show that Kennedy's limo slowed or stopped after the shooting started on Elm Street. Does this indicate Zapruder film fakery, Secret Service involvement in a plot, or poor performance on the part of driver Will Greer? Read it, and decide.

The Babushka Lady is a nickname for an unknown woman who might have filmed the presidential motorcade during the John F. Kennedy assassination. She was called the Babushka Lady by investigators because she wore a scarf similar to a Russian babushka. She appeared to be filming with something like an amateur movie camera.

She was in turn filmed by others, proving her presence on the square, but it is not positively known who she was and why she was filming the president, though many onlookers with cameras were in Dealey Plaza that day. She never came forward. Police and FBI did not find her, and the film shot from her position never turned up.

In 1970, a woman called Beverly Oliver came forward and claimed to be the Babushka Lady. Though she released a memoir chronicling the events of the day of Kennedy's assassination, she has not been able to provide convincing proof she was there. Oliver says her film was taken by an unidentified agent who promised to return it. Critics have noted a number of inconsistencies with her story, such as her use of a type of camera which did not exist in 1963. (*)

(*) Source: (see page 124)

Chapter VII

JFK Legacy

Television coverage gave us information:

Television became the primary source by which people were kept informed of events surrounding John F. Kennedy's assassination. Newspapers were kept as souvenirs rather than sources of updated information. In this sense it was the first major "TV news event" of its kind, the TV coverage uniting the nation, interpreting what went on and creating memories of this space in time. All three major U.S. Television networks suspended their regular schedules and switched to all-news coverage from November 22 through November 25, 1963, being on the air for not more than 70 hours, and it was the longest uninterrupted news event on American TV until 9/11. The record was broken only just before 13:00 UTC, September 14, 2001, by which time the networks had been on for 72 hours straight, covering the terror attacks on the World Trade Center and Pentagon. Kennedy's State Funeral procession and the murder of Lee Harvey Oswald were all broadcast live in America and in other places around the World. The State Funeral was the first of three in a span of 12 months: The other two were for General Douglas MacArthur and Herbert Hoover.

The assassination had an effect on many people, not only in the U.S. but also among the world population. Many vividly remember where they were when first learning of the news that Kennedy was assassinated, as with the Japanese attack on Pearl Harbor on December 7, 1941 before it and the September 11 attacks after it. U.N. Ambassador Adlai Stevenson said of the assassination: "all of us... will bear the grief of his death until the day of ours." Many people have also spoken of the shocking news, compounded by the pall of uncertainty about the identity of the assassin(s), the possible instigators and the causes of the killing as an end to innocence, and in retrospect it has been coalesced with other changes of the tumultuous decade of the 1960s, especially the Vietnam War.

Special Forces have a special bond with Kennedy. "It was President Kennedy who was responsible for the rebuilding of the Special Forces and giving us back our Green Beret," said Forrest Lindley, a writer for the newspaper Stars and Stripes who served with Special Forces in Vietnam. This bond was shown at JFK's funeral. At the commemoration of the 25th anniversary of JFK's death, Gen. Michael D. Healy, the last commander of Special Forces in Vietnam, spoke at Arlington Cemetery. Later, a wreath in the form of the Green Beret would be placed on the grave, continuing a tradition that began the day of his funeral when a sergeant in charge of a detail of Special Forces men guarding the grave placed his beret on the coffin. (cont.)

Political and historical importance:

Ultimately, the death of President Kennedy and the ensuing confusion surrounding the facts of his assassination are of Political and historical importance insofar as they marked a turning point and decline in the faith of the American people in the political establishment—a point made by commentators from Gore Vidal to Arthur M. Schlesinger, Jr. and implied by Oliver Stone in several of his films. Kennedy's continuation of Presidents Harry S. Truman's and Dwight D. Eisenhower's policies of giving economic and military aid to the Vietnam War preceded President Johnson's escalation of the conflict. This contributed to a decade of national difficulties and disappointment on the political landscape. Many of Kennedy's speeches (especially his inaugural address) are considered iconic; and despite his relatively short term in office and lack of major legislative changes coming to fruition during his term, Americans regularly vote him as one of the best presidents, in the same league as Abraham Lincoln, George Washington, and Franklin D. Roosevelt. Some excerpts of Kennedy's inaugural address are engraved on a plaque at his grave at Arlington.

He was posthumously awarded the Pacem in Terris Award. It was named after a 1963 encyclical letter by Pope John XXIII that calls upon all people of goodwill to secure peace among all nations. Pacem in Terris is Latin for 'Peace on Earth.' President Kennedy is the only President to have predeceased both his mother and father. He is also the only President to have predeceased a grandparent. His grandmother, Mary Josephine Hannon Fitzgerald, died in 1964, just over eight months after his assassination.

Civil Rights

The turbulent end of State-sanctioned racial discrimination was one of the most pressing domestic issues of Kennedy's era. The United States Supreme Court had ruled in 1954 in **Brown v. Board of Education** that racial segregation in Public Schools was unconstitutional. However, many Schools, especially in Southern States, did not obey the Supreme Court's judgment. Segregation on buses, in restaurants, movie theaters, bathrooms, and other public places remained. Kennedy supported Racial Integration and Civil Rights, and during the 1960 Campaign he telephoned Coretta Scott King, wife of the Jailed Reverend Martin Luther King, Jr., which perhaps drew some additional Black support to his Candidacy. John and Robert Kennedy's intervention secured the early release of King from Jail. (cont.)

Civil Rights (cont.)

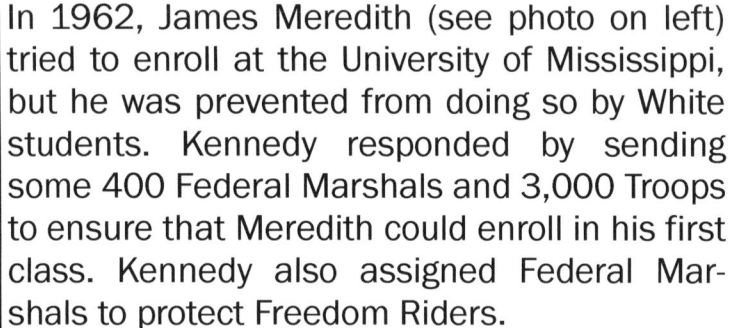

In 1962, James Meredith (see photo on left) tried to enroll at the University of Mississippi, but he was prevented from doing so by White students. Kennedy responded by sending some 400 Federal Marshals and 3,000 Troops to ensure that Meredith could enroll in his first class. Kennedy also assigned Federal Marshals to protect Freedom Riders.

As President, Kennedy initially believed the grassroots Movement for Civil Rights would only anger many Southern Whites and make it even more difficult to pass Civil Rights Laws through Congress, which was dominated by conservative Southern Democrats, and he distanced himself from it. As a result, many Civil Rights leaders viewed Kennedy as unsupportive of their efforts.

On June 11, 1963, President Kennedy intervened when Alabama Governor George Wallace blocked the doorway to the University of Alabama to stop two African American students, Vivian Malone and James Hood, from enrolling. George Wallace moved aside after being confronted by Federal Marshals, Deputy Attorney General Nicholas Katzenbach and the Alabama National Guard. That evening Kennedy gave his famous Civil Rights address on National Television and Radio. Kennedy proposed what would become the Civil Rights Act of 1964.

Kennedy signed the Executive Order creating the Presidential Commission on the Status of Women in 1961. Commission statistics revealed that women were also experiencing discrimination. Their final Report documenting legal and cultural barriers was issued in October 1963, a month before Kennedy's assassination. (*)

(*) Source: (see page 124)

John F. Kennedy Quotes:

- "And so, my fellow Americans. . .ask not what your Country can do for you. . .ask what you can do for your Country. My fellow Citizens of the World. . .ask not what America will do for you, but what together we can do for the Freedom of Man."

- "I do not promise to consider Race or Religion in my appointments. I promise only that I will not consider them."

- "Hungry men and women cannot wait for economic discussions or diplomatic meetings -- and their hunger rests heavily on the consciences of their fellow men."

- "Let us not seek the Republican answer or the Democratic answer but the right answer."

- "Man holds in his mortal hands the power to abolish all forms of human poverty and all forms of human life."

- "When written in Chinese, the word 'crisis' is composed of two characters -- one represents danger and one represents opportunity."

- "While we shall negotiate freely, we shall not negotiate freedom."

- "I believe in human dignity as the source of National purpose, human liberty as the source of National action, the human heart as the source of national compassion, and in the human mind as the source of our invention and our ideas."

- "With a good conscience our only sure reward, with history the final judge of our deeds, let us go forth to lead the land we love, asking His blessing and His help, but knowing that here on Earth God's work must truly be our own."

- "We seek not the World-wide victory of one Nation or System but a World-wide victory of man. The modern Globe is too small, its weapons too destructive, and its disorders too contagious to permit any other kind of victory."

- "I do not believe that any of us would exchange places with any other people or any other generation. The energy, the faith, the devotion which we bring to this endeavor will light our Country and all who serve it -- and the glow from that fire can truly light the World." (*)

(*) Source: (see page 124)

The Kennedy Tragedies:

Behind the glamorous facade, the Kennedys also experienced many personal tragedies. Jacqueline had a miscarriage in 1955 and a stillbirth in 1956. Their newborn son, Patrick Bouvier Kennedy, died in August 1963. Kennedy had two children who survived infancy. One of the fundamental aspects of the Kennedy family is a tragic strain which has run through the family, as a result of the violent and untimely deaths of many of its members. John's eldest brother, Joseph P. Kennedy, Jr., died in World War II, at the age of 29. It was Joe Jr. who was originally to carry the family's hopes for the Presidency. Then both John himself, and his brother Robert died as a result of assassinations. Edward had brushes with death, the first in a Plane crash and the second as a result of a car accident, known as the Chappaquiddick incident. Edward Kennedy died at age 77, on August 25, 2009, from the effects of a malignant brain tumor.

The Kennedy tragedies, colloquially called the Kennedy Curse, is a term sometimes used to describe a series of tragedies involving members of the Kennedy family. Some have called the continual misfortune of the Kennedy family a curse. Several members of the family have died from unnatural causes, most notably brothers John and Robert, who were assassinated by gunshots in 1963 and 1968, and John, Jr., who was killed in an Airplane crash along with his wife and sister-in-law in 1999.

The existence of such a curse has been disputed by others who have claimed that many of the tragedies have been caused by preventable reckless choices like driving drunk or flying an airplane in unsafe conditions, or by specifically choosing relatively dangerous careers such as military service or politics. They contend that if such events were to be subtracted from the Kennedy family record, then what remains would resemble a more ordinary table of events likely to occur in such a large family, such as cancer or pregnancy miscarriage. Some further contend that the notion of a curse is superstitious and is created and fostered by the Media.

Chronology:

Believers in the curse generally cite the following core events as evidence of the family's misfortunes:

- 1941 – Rosemary Kennedy was believed to be mentally retarded. However, some sources have claimed she was suffering from mental illness, such as depression. Because of her increasingly violent and severe mood swings, her father, Joseph Sr., arranged in secret for her to undergo a lobotomy. The surgery impaired her cognitive abilities even more, and as a result, she remained Institutionalized until her death in 2005.

- August 12, 1944 – Joseph P. Kennedy, Jr. is killed in action in a mid-air Aircraft explosion over Eastern England while flying a hazardous mission during World War II.

(cont.)

Chronology: (cont.)

- May 13, 1948 – Kathleen Cavendish, Marchioness of Hartington is killed in a Plane crash in France along with her companion, Peter Wentworth-Fitzwilliam, 8th Earl Fitzwilliam
- August 23, 1956 – Jacqueline Bouvier Kennedy gives birth to their stillborn daughter, Arabella. (Although the daughter was unnamed and is buried at Arlington National Cemetery next to her parents with a marker reading "Daughter", later reports indicated that the Kennedys had intended to name her Arabella.)
- August 9, 1963 – Patrick Bouvier Kennedy, born six weeks premature, dies two days after his birth.
- November 22, 1963 – U.S. President John F. Kennedy is assassinated, in Dallas, Texas.
- June 19, 1964 – U.S. Senator Ted Kennedy is involved in a Plane crash in which one of his aides and the Pilot were killed. He was pulled from the wreckage by fellow Senator Birch E. Bayh II and spent weeks in a Hospital recovering from a broken back, a punctured lung, broken ribs, and internal bleeding.
- June 6, 1968 – U.S. Senator Robert F. Kennedy is assassinated by Sirhan Sirhan in Los Angeles immediately following his victory in the California Democratic Presidential Primary.
- July 18, 1969 – In the Chappaquiddick incident, a car driven by Ted Kennedy goes off a bridge on Martha's Vineyard, eventually drowning his passenger Mary Jo Kopechne. In his July 25 televised statement, Kennedy stated that on the night of the incident he wondered *"whether some awful curse did actually hang over all the Kennedys."*
- August 13, 1973 – Joseph P. Kennedy II is the driver in a car accident that leaves one passenger, Pam Kelley, permanently paralyzed.
- November 17, 1973 – Edward M. Kennedy, Jr. loses a portion of his right leg due to bone cancer at the age of 12.
- April 25, 1984 – David Anthony Kennedy dies from a Demerol and Cocaine overdose in a Palm Beach, Florida Hotel room.
- December 31, 1997 – Michael LeMoyne Kennedy is killed in a skiing accident in Aspen, Colorado.
- July 16, 1999 – John F. Kennedy, Jr. is killed in a Plane crash along with his wife Carolyn and sister-in-law when the Piper Saratoga light Aircraft he was piloting crashed into the Atlantic Ocean off the Coast of Martha's Vineyard due to Pilot error and foggy weather. They were on their way to a relative wedding. (*)

(*) Source: (see page 124)

Presidents Assassinated in Office:

Abraham Lincoln: (1809-1865)

The assassination of Abraham Lincoln took place on Good Friday, April 14, 1865, at approximately 10:15 pm. Lincoln was shot by an actor and Confederate sympathizer John Wilkes Booth while attending a performance of *Our American Cousin* at Ford's Theatre with his wife, Mary Todd Lincoln, and two guests. Soon after being shot, Lincoln's wound was declared to be mortal. Lincoln died the following day at 7:22 am.

Booth was tracked down by Union soldiers and was shot and killed by Sergeant Boston Corbett on April 26, 1865. This is an example of a politically-motivated assassination, since Booth believed that killing Lincoln would radically change U.S. policy toward the South. (*)

James A. Garfield: (1831-1881)

The assassination of James A. Garfield took place in Washington, D.C., at 9:30 am on Saturday, July 2, 1881, less than four months after Garfield took office. Charles J. Guiteau shot him with a .442 Webley British Bulldog revolver. Garfield died 11 weeks later, on Monday, September 19, 1881, at 10:35 pm, due to complications caused by infections.

Guiteau was immediately arrested. He was tried and found guilty. He appealed, but his appeal was rejected, and he was hanged on June 30, 1882 in the District of Columbia. Guiteau was almost certainly mentally unbalanced, but the shooting was motivated by Guiteau's beliefs. (*)

William McKinley: (1843-1901)

The assassination of William McKinley took place at 4:07 pm on Friday, September 6, 1901, at the Temple of Music in Buffalo, New York. McKinley, attending the Pan-American Exposition, was shot twice by Leon Czolgosz, an anarchist. McKinley died eight days later, on September 14, 1901, at 2:15 am.

Members of the crowd immediately subdued Czolgosz after he shot McKinley. Afterwards, the 4th Brigade, National Guard Signal Corps, and Police intervened and beat him so severely it was initially thought he might not live to stand trial. Czolgosz did survive and was convicted and sentenced to death on September 23. Czolgosz was electrocuted by three jolts, each of 1800 volts, in Auburn Prison on October 29, 1901. Czolgosz's actions were politically motivated, although it is unclear what outcome he believed the shooting would yield. (*)

(*) Source: (see page 124)

Chapter VIII

JFK's Funeral

President Kennedy casket:

A last kiss to say good by:

(*) Source: (see page 124)

Pennsylvania Avenue:

(*) Source: (see page 124)

Leader of the Nation supporting the Kennedy family:

Dr Martin Luther King Jr.

MLK Jr.   RFK   LBJ

(*) Source: (see page 124)

First burial site and Church service of John F. Kennedy:

On November 25, 1963, John F. Kennedy's body was buried in a small plot, (20 by 30 ft.), in Arlington National Cemetery (see above photo). Over a period of 3 years, (1964–1966), an estimated 16 million people had visited his grave.

On March 14, 1967, Kennedy's body was moved to a permanent burial plot and memorial at the Cemetery. The Funeral was officiated by Father John J Cavanaugh. The Honor Guard at JFK`s graveside was the 37th Cadet Class of the Irish Army. JFK was greatly impressed by the Irish Cadets on his last official visit to the Republic of Ireland, so much so that Jackie Kennedy requested the Irish Army to be the Honor Guard at the Funeral.

Kennedy final resting place is in Arlington National Cemetery. Kennedy's wife, Jacqueline and their two deceased minor children were buried with him later. His brother, Senator Robert Kennedy, was buried nearby in June 1968. In August 2009, his brother, Senator Edward M. Kennedy, was also buried near his two brothers.

Kennedy and William Howard Taft are the only two U.S. Presidents buried at Arlington. (*)

(*) Source: (see page 124)

Kennedy wife accept his flag:

(*) Source: (see page 124)

John F. Kennedy Eternal Flame (final resting place):

(*) Source: (see page 124)

Honors to John F. Kennedy:

- John F. Kennedy International Airport, American facility (renamed from Idlewild in December 1963) in New York City's Queens County; Nation's busiest International Gateway.

- John F. Kennedy Memorial Airport American facility in Ashland County, Wisconsin, near City of Ashland.

- John F. Kennedy Memorial Bridge American seven-lane transportation hub across Ohio River; completed in late 1963, the bridge links Kentucky and Indiana.

- John F. Kennedy School of Government, American Institution (renamed from Harvard Graduate School of Public Administration in 1966).

- John F. Kennedy Space Center, U.S. Government Installation that manages and operates America's astronaut launch facilities.

- John F. Kennedy University, American private educational Institution founded in California in 1964; locations in Pleasant Hill, Campbell, Berkeley, and Santa Cruz.

- USS John F. Kennedy (CV-67), U.S. Navy Aircraft Carrier ordered in April 1964, launched May 1967, decommissioned August 2007; nicknamed "Big John".

- John F. Kennedy High School is the name of many Secondary Schools.

- Kennedy received a signet ring engraved with his Arms for his 44th birthday as a gift from his wife, and the Arms were incorporated into the Seal of the USS John F. Kennedy. Following his assassination, Kennedy was honored by the Canadian Government by having a mountain, Mount Kennedy, named for him, which his brother, Robert Kennedy, climbed in 1965 to plant a banner of the Arms at the summit. (*)

(*) Source: (see page 124)

Chapter IX

JFK Last Speech in Ft. Worth

JFK's Last Night at Hotel Texas 1963 Fort Worth, TX

Registered as a National historic landmark, the Hilton Fort Worth Hotel has welcomed many famous and important Guests. None would prove to be more significant than President John F. Kennedy and the First Lady, Jacqueline. Using the Hotel as a backdrop, the young President addressed the thousands who had gathered to catch a glimpse of America's most popular political figure. His final speech came minutes later in the Hotel's Crystal Ballroom where 2,000 attendees joined the President and First Lady for breakfast. In only a few short hours the Hilton Fort Worth Hotel in Texas would go down in history as the place where President John F. Kennedy spent his last night. (cont.)

"There are no faint hearts in Fort Worth" - President John F. Kennedy, November 22, 1963.

Address:
Hilton Hotel
815 Main Street
Fort Worth, TX 76102

Art in JFK and first lady Fort Worth Suite:

This Nov. 22, 1963 photo provided by the Amon Carter Museum of American Art shows the paintings Thomas Eakins' Swimming and Charles M. Russell's Lost in a Snowstorm that were installed in in Suite 850 at the Hotel Texas in Fort Worth, where the President and first lady stayed the night before their trip to Dallas.

President Kennedy and First Lady Jacqueline Bouvier Kennedy spent the night in Fort Worth before arriving in Dallas for the Motorcade Parade on Nov. 22, 1963. Featuring paintings by Vincent van Gogh, Thomas Eakins, Lyonel Feininger, Franz Kline and Marsden Hartley and sculptures by Pablo Picasso and Henry Moore, the artwork adorned Presidential Suite 850, courtesy of a small group of Fort Worth collectors.

"*Hotel Texas: An Art Exhibition for the President and Mrs. John F. Kennedy*" will debut at the DMA on May 26, 2013 and run through Sept. 15, 2013, under the title "**Hotel Texas: An Art Exhibition for the President and Mrs. John F. Kennedy**." Organizers say they hope to "*reveal for the first time the complete story of the Presidential Suite 850 installation ... and examine the significance of art both to the Kennedys and to the Dallas-Fort Worth Communities.*"

DMA director Maxwell Anderson issued a prepared statement, saying that the "*Exhibition provides an unprecedented opportunity to rediscover the Kennedys' time in Texas, prior to the untimely death of the President, and to enhance our understanding of how the President and First Lady were perceived at that point in History. The Organization of an Art Exhibition for the couple was a testament to their appreciation for the Arts. It also underscored*

The morning of November 22, 1963:

On the morning of Nov. 22, 1963, President John F. Kennedy and First Lady Jacqueline Kennedy realized that their **Fort Worth Hotel** Suite featured an extraordinary array of artwork — from a painting by Vincent van Gogh to a bronze by Pablo Picasso.

A group of prominent Fort Worth citizens had scrambled to put together the collection in the days leading up to the President's fateful Texas visit, transforming an otherwise plain suite into something special.

Next year, almost all of those works the couple admired in their last private moments before President Kennedy was assassinated will be on display at an exhibit that opens at the Dallas Museum of Art in commemoration of the 50th anniversary of his death.

"It's not a story about death. It's not a story about hate. It's a story about art and love, which I think is a very good tribute to the Kennedys. It's all about their love of Art," said Olivier Meslay, Associate Director of curatorial affairs at the Museum and the exhibit's Curator.

Before the Kennedys' visit, Fort Worth newspapers had revealed details about the preparations, including the description of the unremarkable Suite 850 at the Hotel Texas, said Scott Grant Barker, a Texas Art Historian who has researched the events. He said that a local Art Critic decided something needed to be done to make the Suite shine. (*)

(*) Source: (see page 124)

JFK making speech to crowd morning of November 22, 1963:

(*) Source: (see page 124)

The crowds in Fort Worth came to greet John F. Kennedy:

(*) Source: (see page 124)

John F. Kennedy Memorial in Fort Worth, Texas:

(*) Source: (see page 124)

The 50th: Honoring the Memory of John F. Kennedy Unspoken Speech in Dallas:

Trammell Crow makes the announcement at Dallas Trade Mart that President Kennedy has been shot on November 22, 1963.

President Kennedy's empty seat at the Dallas Trade Mart on Nov. 22, 1963.

Devastation spread across the Nation on November 22, 1963, when President John F. Kennedy was killed by an assassin's bullet in Dallas, Texas. President Kennedy was en route here to the Dallas Trade Mart, to speak to 2,600 guests of the Dallas Business Community, when he was assassinated at Dealey Plaza by Lee Harvey Oswald. Guests were anxiously awaiting the arrival of the President accompanied by his lovely wife Jackie, when Dallas Market Center owner and developer Trammell Crow delivered the tragic news that the President had been shot on the way to the luncheon. The event was one of Dallas's greatest tragedies.

Fifty years later, we have not forgotten the events of this day. In remembrance of the speech that President Kennedy was unable to make that day in Dallas.

The Unspoken Speech Project was developed. The Community-driven project allows citizens of Dallas to honor President Kennedy, by delivering the speech in unique ways, one word and one citizen at a time. Seven installments craft individual segments of the speech to complete the *Unspoken Speech*. The last installment, **"Lord Keep The City"** features the South Dallas Concert Choir singing the conclusion of Kennedy's speech here at the Dallas Trade Mart, in the exact same spot that Kennedy was to deliver it. (*)

(*) Source: (see page 124)

Chapter X

CIA Director withheld Information about JFK Death

CIA Headquarters: Langley, Fairfax County, Virginia

CIA Director withheld information about JFK: (update 2015)

LANGLEY, Va., Oct. 13, 2015 (UPI) -- A declassified CIA Report reveals former Director John McCone (see photo on left) withheld information to the Warren Commission investigating the assassination of President John F. Kennedy.

A Secret Report written in 2013 by CIA historian David Robarge (see middle photo) and declassified in fall of 2014, alleges McCone led a "*benign cover up*" that kept "*incendiary*" information about the CIA from the Warren Commission, the Report said. McCone's cover up was designed to keep the Commission focused on "*what the Agency believed was the 'best truth' - that Lee Harvey Oswald, ... acted alone in killing John Kennedy,*" the Report said.

McCone withheld the existence of years of CIA plots to work with the Mafia to assassinate Fidel Castro. Had that been known by the Commission, it would have raised the question of whether Oswald truly acted alone or if he might have worked with Cuba or the Soviet Union.

But Robarge asserts that McCone was convinced that Oswald had acted alone and directed the Agency to only provide "*passive, reactive and selective*" assistance to the Commission.

Robarge told **Politico**, the Agency had declassified the Report "*to highlight misconceptions about the CIA's connection to JFK's assassination.*" A common conspiracy theory is that the CIA was in some way behind the killing.

President Lyndon Johnson created the Warren Commission in 1963 to investigate the murder of Kennedy. The Commission found that Oswald acted alone in the assassination and the McCone revelations might not have changed that, but would have been potentially disastrous to the Spy Agency.

Among the most important information McCone and other Officials failed to divulge was that the CIA had spent years plotting the assassination of Fidel Castro (see bottom photo).

Not being aware of these plots, the Warren Commission could not know that was something to investigate — but the new information suggests it would have been valuable. (cont.)

CIA Director withheld information: (cont.)

While living in New Orleans in 1963, for example, Oswald shared office space with a CIA-backed anti-Castro group. Oswald had handed out pro-Castro literature with the address 544 Camp Street on it. FBI Agent Guy Bannister (see photo on left) and a CIA-backed Cuban Revolutionary Council also rented space at the same location.

"One thing that I've always wondered about is [Oswald's] time in New Orleans because he was apparently associated with Guy Bannister, who clearly had FBI and CIA ties, and yet he's also scuffling on the Street with [the local Representative of] an anti-Castro group," Sabato told **Business Insider** in 2013.

And Sabato's book notes that "*it could be that Oswald was just a Forrest-Gump like character who popped up at interesting moments wherever he happened to live.* "But just as conceivably, whether related to the Kennedy assassination or not, Oswald actually had secretive contacts with the CIA or the FBI, or both*," he said.

Continuing the lie:

The Report also reveals that in 1978, McCone lied about failing to divulge the Castro plots. When the House Committee asked him whether the Spy Agency had withheld information from the Commission about the plots to kill Castro, McCone said he couldn't answer because he had not been told about the plots. The Report says that McCone's answer "*was neither frank nor accurate.*"

According to one of the Lawyers of the Warren Commission cited in the Report, McCone had discussed Robert Kennedy's (see photo on left) uneasiness about the CIA withholding that information in 1975.The U.S. Attorney General at the time of his brother's assassination, Robert Kennedy had been overseeing the Spy Agency's anti-Castro actions, which included some of the assassination plots.

According to the Report, McCone thought that "**Robert Kennedy had personal feelings of guilt because he was directly or indirectly involved with the anti-Castro planning.**" The Report hints at the kind of questions the President's brother might have been asking himself, namely: "**Had the Administration's obsession with Cuba inadvertently inspired a politicized sociopath to murder John Kennedy?**" (cont.)

Continuing the lie: (cont.)

Although the Report sheds some light on the extent of a CIA cover-up, it still leaves many questions unanswered. Numerous names and mentions throughout the Report have also been redacted, suggesting that some information might never be publicly disclosed.

And as to whether Oswald acted alone or with accomplices, those who doubt the Warren Commission's findings might never find a satisfying answer. *"For all attempts to close the case as 'just Oswald,' fair-minded observers continue to be troubled by many aspects of eyewitness testimony and paper trails,"* Sabato writes.

The Report concludes that McCone could only be accused of being a *"co-conspirator"* in a cover-up surrounding Kennedy's assassination insofar as he kept the conspiracy to kill Castro secret after November 22, 1964. *"As far as the CIA goes ... it is clear beyond question that the CIA lied repeatedly to the Warren Commission and continued lying to the House Select Committee on Assassinations,"* Sabato said in 2013.

"Revealing nothing about the assassination attempts on Fidel Castro. Revealing very little about the fact they kept close tabs on Oswald: They knew what he was doing, they were evaluating him. I think they had something in mind. I don't subscribe to the hidden coup within the CIA, although I don't rule it out."

The CIA recently told **Politico** that the Agency decided to declassify the Report *"to highlight misconceptions about the CIA's connection to JFK's assassination,"* including the infamous **"Grassy Knoll"** (see above photo) theory that asserts the CIA was behind the assassination.

New details could come out when thousands of CIA Documents are scheduled to be released in October 2017.

Said Sabato: *"The President at that time will get to rule whether anything can remain secret and redacted."* (*) (Follow up information in 2017)

(*) Source: (see page 124)

The Umbrella Man:

On the 48th anniversary of Kennedy's murder, the *Times* ran an op-ed piece and short film by documentary maker Errol Morris about another man's research into *"umbrella man."* Umbrella Man is the nickname for a fellow who famously brought an umbrella on a sunny day for the President's visit to Dallas November 22, 1963, stood on the **"Grassy Knoll,"** and, just as the President's car passed, he opened the umbrella and pumped it in the air. Many have speculated as to the significance, or lack of significance, of this strange behavior. Some wonder if Umbrella Man was part of the assassination scenario, perhaps signaling to shooters.

There was even the September 1975 Senate Intelligence Committee testimony by Charles Senseney, a contract weapons designer for the CIA, that the Agency had perfected an umbrella that shoots undetectable poison darts that can immobilize and kill, raising questions about whether this was in play that day. (See P. 168 in the Senate Committee testimony, where Senseney explains specifically about the Agency's use of a toxin and the ability to fire it from a modified umbrella.)

The self-described Umbrella Man, Louie Steven Witt (see on next page), came forward to offer his testimony in 1978, or three years after the CIA expert provided this now forgotten testimony on umbrellas as weapon. Umbrella Man came forward just as a special House Select Committee on Assassinations was focusing on the possibility of a conspiracy (which, it concluded in its final report...was likely.) (You can order a video of a report on Witt's testimony, by then **ABC News** reporter Brit Hume, here)

The Counsel for the Assassinations Committee, remarkably, does not mention the prior Senate testimony by the CIA weapons expert that such an umbrella device did exist, and instead quotes a more shaky claim by an *"assassinations critic"* regarding such a device.

Instead, the Morris video presents the idea that sometimes, the most ridiculous scenarios are the truth. And so it presents the ridiculous, and asks us to believe it. Cutting to the chase, the man seen opening an umbrella comes forward to explain why he did it. Reason: in 1963, he was still mad at Britain's pre-War Prime Minister Neville Chamberlain and his appeasement of Hitler, and held JFK's father to blame as U.S. Ambassador to England in that Period. Chamberlain was famed for carrying an umbrella. So—get this—Umbrella Man, hoping to make a statement about what happened in the late 1930s to JFK in 1963, pumped his umbrella at the time the fatal shots were fired...only for this obscure purpose. (cont.)

The Umbrella Man: (cont.)

Here are some things you should know about the man who came forward to identify himself as Umbrella Man and tell this ludicrous Neville Chamberlain story:

> His account of his activities that day don't track with what Umbrella Man actually did, raising questions as to whether this man who volunteered to testify to the assassination inquiry is even the real umbrella-bearer, or someone whose purpose was to end inquiries into the matter.

> The man who came forward, Louie Steven Witt (see photo on left), was a young man at the time of Kennedy's death. How many young men in Dallas in 1963 even knew what Neville Chamberlain had done a quarter-Century before?

> In 1963, Witt was an insurance salesman for the Rio Grande National Life Insurance company, which anchored the eponymous Rio Grande Building in Downtown Dallas. It's an interesting building. Among the other outfits housed in the building was the Office of Immigration and Naturalization—a place Lee Harvey Oswald visited repeatedly upon his return from Russia, ostensibly to deal with matters concerning the Immigration status of his Russian-born wife, Marina. Another occupant of the Rio Grande Building was the U.S. Secret Service, so notably lax in its protection of Kennedy that day, breaking every rule of security on every level.

A major client of Rio Grande was the U.S. Military, to which it provided insurance. It's worth considering the roles of Military-connected figures on the day of the assassination. These include Dallas Military Intelligence unit Chief Jack Crichton operating secretly from an underground communications bunker; Crichton's providing a translator who twisted Marina Oswald's statement to Police in a way that implicated her husband; and members of Military Intelligence forcing their way into the pilot car of Kennedy's motorcade, which inexplicably ground to a halt in front of the Texas School Book Depository (where Lee Harvey Oswald's employer, a high Official with the local Military-connected American Legion, managed to find a "job" for Oswald at a time when his company was otherwise seasonally laying off staff.) Oh, and it's worth contemplating JFK's titanic, if under-reported, struggle with Top Pentagon Officials over how the U.S. should interact with Russia, Cuba, and the rest of the World. You can read more about all this in my book *Family of Secrets*.

Is this concatenation of facts too crazy to consider? More crazy than that Neville Chamberlain story? (*)

(*) Source: (see page 124)

Oswald's Raleigh Call:

One of the most interesting and potentially important aspects of the John Kennedy assassination may not have anything to do with the murder itself. A story concerning the actions of the accused assassin, Lee Harvey Oswald, has simmered on the back burner of the investigation since its discovery ten years ago, and is considered by leading assassination authorities to be a key in the unsolved mystery.

Oswald's movements and statements inside the Dallas jail up to the time of his murder have always been a huge mystery, and any clues to what happened during that time are vigorously sought by all researchers. So when a story surfaced that Oswald attempted to place a call from the Jail to a person whose name had not otherwise entered the assassination investigation, it was big news.

In short, it is alleged that Oswald attempted to place a call to a John Hurt in Raleigh, North Carolina on Saturday evening, November 23, 1963, but was mysteriously prevented from completing the call. Though there is speculation that the call was incoming rather than outgoing (for example, a crank call to the Jail from someone by that name), private and Congressional researchers believe Oswald, for whatever reasons, was the one attempting the call. The implications of that call have prompted former U.S. Intelligence Officials to speculate on Oswald's possible link with Intelligence Agencies.

How We Know What We Know:

On the night of November 23, 1963, two telephone operators were working the switchboard that controlled, among other Dallas Municipal Offices, the Jail. One of the ladies, Mrs. Alveeta A. Treon, made a statement concerning the events of that night to assassination researcher and Attorney Bernard Fensterwald some five years after the assassination, but then refused to sign it on advice from her Lawyer, according to Fensterwald. The following is a condensation of that statement:

Mrs. Treon arrived for work at the switchboard between 10:15 and 10:35 that evening, and was told by her fellow worker, Mrs. Louise Swinney, that their supervisor had asked them to assist Law enforcement officials to listen to a call that Lee Harvey Oswald would be making soon. Two men, that Mrs. Treon thinks might have been Secret Service Agents, subsequently came into the switchboard area and were put in an adjacent room where they could monitor the expected call. (cont.)

Oswald's Raleigh Call: (cont.)

At about 10:45 pm, the call from the Jail came through, and both ladies rushed to take it. Mrs. Swinney handled the call, as it turned out; wrote down the information on the number Oswald wished to reach; and notified the two men of the call. Quoting from Mrs. Treon's statement: "*I was dumbfounded at what happened next. Mrs. Swinney opened the key to Oswald and told him, 'I'm sorry, the number doesn't answer.' She then unplugged and disconnected Oswald without ever really trying to put the call through. A few moments later, Mrs. Swinney tore the page off her notation pad and threw it into the wastepaper basket.*" After Mrs. Swinney left work at approximately 11:00 pm, Mrs. Treon retrieved the piece of paper, and copied the information from it onto a telephone slip commonly used by the operators to record calls, so that she could keep it as a "*souvenir*."

That slip, which would turn up seven years later in a Freedom of Information Suit brought by Chicago researcher Sherman H. Skolnick (a Civil action filed in Federal District Court in Chicago, April 6, 1970, No. 70C 790), contains some startling things. It purports to show a collect call attempted from the Jail by Lee Harvey Oswald to a John Hurt at 919-834-7430 and it gives another telephone number in the 919 Area Code, 833-1253. (The slip is reproduced in the Appendix of the 1975 book, Coup d'Etat in America by Canfield and Weberman, the first major work to deal with the "*Raleigh call*" and its implications for Oswald's links to Intelligence Agencies.) What do we know about those two telephone numbers? The House Assassinations Committee gave one of its Staffers, Surell Brady, responsibility for investigating the "Raleigh Call." Though the Committee's final report did not mention the call, Brady wrote a 28-page internal memorandum out ling the results of their investigation of the incident.

In an insert after page 15 of the document, it is incorrectly reported that the two numbers listed on the telephone slip "were unpublished in 1963." This information was reported as having been supplied by Carolyn Rabon of Southern Bell Telephone Co. in 1978. However, a simple check of the December, 1962 Southern Bell telephone directory for Raleigh, North Carolina (which would have been current at the time of the assassination) and the December, 1963 directory (which would contain any new information and reflect any changes of listing status) shows that both numbers were published. Thus, both of these numbers would have been available to anyone calling "Information" in Raleigh, asking for a John Hurt. This is the way the listings appear in those directories: DECEMBER, 1962: Hurt John D 415 New Bern Av TE4-7430; Hurt John W Old Wake Forest Rd 833-1253; DECEMBER, 1963: Hurt John D 201 Hillsbro 834-7430; Hurt John W Old Wake Forest Rd 833-1253 Why Southern Bell would have provided incorrect information, or how they could have made such a gross mistake, is uncertain. (cont.)

Oswald's Raleigh Call: (cont.)

Who Is John Hurt?

Obviously, the identity of any person whom Lee Harvey Oswald might have attempted to contact after having been arrested for the murder of the President would be of immense interest. Other than identifying the second telephone number as belonging to one "*John W. Hurt of [Old Wake] Forest Road in Raleigh, North Carolina,*" the Brady Report does not supply any information about that number. Subsequent attempts to trace John W. Hurt have proven fruitless. The first number, however, presents less of a mystery. I dialed the number and spoke at some length with a man who identified himself as John David Hurt. (Excerpts from that interview accompany this article.) The most tantalizing aspect of this Mr. Hurt is that he was a U.S. Army Counterintelligence officer during World War II. Mr. Hurt acknowledged this Wartime service, but denied ever having been anything other than an insurance investigator and an employee of the State of North Carolina since the War.

Hurt denied that he made or received a call to or from the Dallas Jail or Lee Harvey Oswald. When asked if he knew of any reason why Lee Harvey Oswald would wish to call him, he said, "*I do not. I never heard of the man before President Kennedy's death.*" Mr. Hurt professed to having been a "*great Kennedyphile,*" and said he "*would have been more inclined to kill*" Oswald than anything else. Asked if he had any explanation as to why his name and telephone number should turn up this way, he said, "*None whatever.*" I also asked him if he had any knowledge of the second phone number on the slip, and he said he had never had that number in his use. "*My number has been the same for, oh, I'd say forty years.*"

If we cannot know who, says Marchetti, we can at least understand why. Whether guilty or not of the assassination, once inside the Dallas Jail Oswald was looking for some way to assure his interrogators, which may well have included Agents of the CIA, according to Marchetti, that he was "*okay.*" If this were true, then one must imagine that Oswald remembered either the name John Hurt in Raleigh, or some other location which got confused with Raleigh, and that either he or someone acting for him obtained the two telephone numbers from "*Information.*" That the call was blocked from going through gives another disturbing, and as yet unsolved, aspect to the case. The importance of the Raleigh call ultimately is that both Marchetti, who is convinced of at least a partial involvement in the assassination by Intelligence Agents, and Blakey, who eschews that explanation as unnecessary, agree that it is an important, disturbing aspect of the JFK case. Said Blakey, "*I consider it unanswered, and I consider the direction in which it went substantiated and disturbing, but ultimately inconclusive.*" When asked if he would recommend that the Justice Department look into the incident, if and when it re-opens the case, Blakey said no. His reason? "*The bottom line is, it's an unanswerable mystery.*" (*)

(*) Source: (see page 124)

10 facts about JFK assassination:

Nov. 22, 2013, marks the 50th anniversary of the assassination of President John F. Kennedy, one of the most momentous and scrutinized moments in American history. Even half a Century later, questions persist: **Who really shot Kennedy?** Was there a conspiracy to kill the President? Why are there still so many loose ends and secrets?

"We analyzed everything we could find, from the facts, to the myths that keep getting repeated," Meltzer says. *"We so want to believe there's a conspiracy. Why? Because we don't want to believe that our Government could be jack-knifed by a High School dropout."*

But sometimes the facts don't line up with the myth. Here, Meltzer shares with Yahoo 10 aspects of the JFK assassination most Americans may not know, whether because they're little-known facts or because the myth is a better story. (cont.)

10 facts about JFK assassination:

10. The window from which Oswald shot Kennedy went missing. On Nov. 22, 1963, Lee Harvey Oswald leaned out a window on the sixth floor of the Texas Book Depository in Dallas and fired three shots. Six years after the assassination, Gen. D. Harold Byrd, owner of the building, had the window removed. *"This being Texas,"* Meltzer says, *"he had it framed and hung in his mansion."* The only problem? It was the wrong window, according to Aubrey Mayhew, the building's later owner. Mayhew pried out what he said was the right window. Both windows eventually ended up on eBay; Meltzer believes Mayhew's is the *"real"* one.

9. Plenty of shooters recreated Oswald's shot. One of the more pervasive myths surrounding the JFK assassination was the idea that no other shooter could replicate Oswald's feat of shooting three times in 6.75 seconds. So another shooter must have been involved, right? Not necessarily. The Warren Commission reported that one marksman was able to pull off the feat in 4.6 seconds, and a later CBS investigation showed that 11 marksmen averaged 5.6 seconds. Also, Oswald's shot was, for a trained shooter, relatively easy. Oswald and other Military marksmen are trained to shoot anywhere from 200 to 500 yards. Kennedy was 88 yards from Oswald at his farthest point, and 59 yards away at the time of the last shot.

8. Oliver Stone's "JFK" damaged history. *"Oliver Stone is a great filmmaker,"* Meltzer says. *"But his film 'JFK' did a great disservice to history by mixing fact and fiction. For the 20 million people that saw it in Theaters, and the millions who have seen it afterward, that became the Official Record of the assassination."* Meltzer notes that several characters in the movie were created for the purposes of storytelling and had no relation whatsoever to real events.

7. There was no "Magic Bullet." The most pervasive myth perpetuated by *"JFK"* was the idea that a single bullet could have passed through Kennedy's body, changed direction twice, and then entered the body of Texas Gov. John Connally, riding in the limo's front seat, before emerging pristine. "You'd think there's no way one bullet could do that, and you'd be right ... if the men were sitting facing forward like they were in an airplane. Governor Connally was turned to the right, and the bullet traveled in a straight line. Also, Meltzer points out, FBI investigators have noted that the bullet is in no way "pristine"; it's flat on one side.

6. The U.S. Government erred in keeping its investigation secret. In 1964, the Warren Commission held the investigation into the assassination behind closed doors. As later review of the proceedings has shown, the absence of publicly released information allowed speculation to spread in many dark (and often incorrect) directions.
(cont.)

10 facts about JFK assassination: (cont.)

5. Kennedy's family chose to keep secrets as well. JFK's family made the understandable, but regrettable, decision to keep Kennedy's hospital and autopsy records under wraps. As with the Warren Commission, Meltzer says, this gave the inaccurate perception that the Kennedy family had something to hide. And it meant the American public didn't get to see the actual evidence.

4. The Government is not keeping very many JFK secrets, and won't keep any for much longer. One benefit of the *JFK* film, Meltzer notes, is that it led to the declassification of 97 percent of all Government documents related to the Kennedy assassination. The other 3 percent will be declassified in 2017, unless the President decides to keep them under wraps.

3. Were there really "mysterious deaths?" One of the pervasive rumors surrounding the investigation into JFK's death was that many witnesses died of mysterious circumstances. Nonsense, Meltzer says. *"The idea that there was a hit squad going around tying off loose ends just doesn't hold up,"* he says. *"Many of the people died long after giving testimony. And most died of heart disease. The No. 1 killer of Americans is heart disease. A few were unusual, but not as many as people say."*

2. There was no "fourth shot" from the Grassy Knoll. The Warren Commission found that there were three shots fired in the assassination. Several years later, the House Select Committee on Assassinations indicated that an audio recording discovered later found that there was a fourth shot, and it must have come from the "Grassy Knoll" near the Depository Building. Problem is, 12 acoustics experts ruled out the possibility of a fourth shot. Moreover, that fourth shot came a minute after Oswald's shots, a time when the Motorcade was already well on the way to the Hospital.

1. The true killer of JFK was ... As Meltzer notes, the *"true killer"* of JFK in the popular imagination changes depending on the mood of the time. *"In the 1960s, we believed it was the Soviets. In the 1970s, it was the CIA, as we distrusted our own Government. In the 1980s, with the rise of Mob movies, it was the Mafia. Now, we believe our own Government was in on it. JFK's killer is whoever we're most afraid of at the time."*

- As both 9/11 and the Boston Marathon bombing have shown, there's no way that a public event could unfurl like the Kennedy assassination, with a lack of primary-source recordings. *"Information travels so quickly now,"* Meltzer says. *"We have camera angles from every direction. All the evidence is right in front of us, all the puzzle pieces are right there."* (*)

(*) Source: (see page 124)

President John F. Kennedy and wife, Jackie Kennedy:

(*) Source: (see page 124)

Walking Tour of Dealey Plaza:

1. **The Grassy Knoll** is on the same side of Elm Street as the Texas School Book Depository and Elm Place, but nearer the overpass. Many witnesses claim they heard shots coming from the Grassy Knoll on the North side of Elm Street.
2. **The Sixth Floor Museum** at Dealey Plaza, where the window has been preserved in an artificial half-opened position. The area inside the window has been recreated to appear as it would have during the shooting. The Museum is open daily from 10 am to 6 pm.
3. **John Neely Bryan Log Cabin** is located at Dallas County Historical Plaza in Downtown Dallas. This small restored log cabin is the home and Trading Post which was erected in 1841 by Dallas founder John Neely Bryan and was the City's first structure.
4. **John F. Kennedy Memorial Plaza** was dedicated June 24, 1970. It is located one block East of Dealey Plaza, between Main and Commerce Streets, on land donated by Dallas County.
5. **The Old Red Museum** was built in 1892 and the red Courthouse contains some of Dallas County's most fascinating historical artifacts. The building's architecture is phenomenal. Dealey Plaza is only a few steps across S. Houston Street from The Old Red Museum of Dallas County History and Culture. The Old Red Museum is open daily from 9 am to 5 pm. (*)

(*) Source: (see page 124)

Walking Tour of Dealey Plaza:

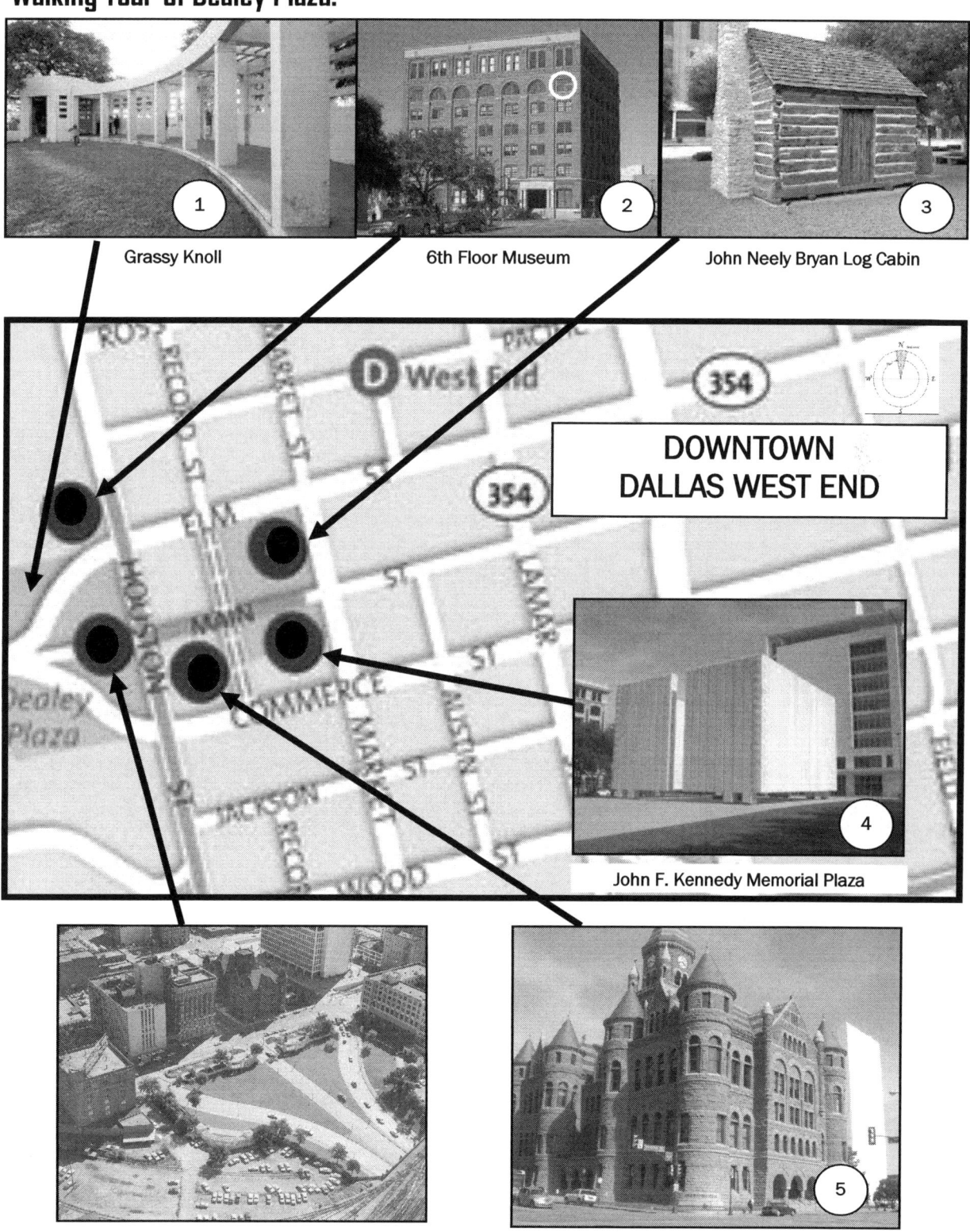

1. Grassy Knoll
2. 6th Floor Museum
3. John Neely Bryan Log Cabin

DOWNTOWN DALLAS WEST END

4. John F. Kennedy Memorial Plaza

Dealey Plaza

5. The Old Red Museum

(*) Source: (see page 124)

Acknowledgements

It would be impossible to list the names of all the people who have contributed in some way to the realization of my research. Without them it would be impossible to gather all the facts and theories and put them in this information book "*Who Really Killed JFK (Facts & Theories)*". I acknowlege and give thanks to Robert Groden for giving me permission to use his photos in my book. I thank all the public records and all free encyclopedia web sites for photos and information that's available, so the public can be informed and educated.

(*) Source:

(*) Source information on each individual or article came from Wikipedia, Google; Yahoo or The Warren Commission Report unless otherwise noted: (*Therlee Gipson*). Each article is only the summary of each individual's life or event. Additional information on these subject matters can be retrieved from Wikipedia, Google, The Warren Commission Report or Yahoo.

Public Domain

The public domain comprises the body of knowledge and innovation (especially creative works such as writing, art, music, and inventions) in relation to which no person or other legal entity can establish or maintain proprietary interests. This body of information and creativity is considered to be part of the common cultural and intellectual heritage of humanity, which in general anyone may use or exploit. If an item is not in the public domain, this may be the result of a proprietary interest as represented by a copyright or patent. The extent to which members of the public may use or exploit an item in relation to which proprietary interests exist is generally limited. However, when copyright or other intellectual property restrictions expire, works will enter the public domain and may be used by anyone.

Content Disclaimer

Inclusion of articles in this book does not mean that the author agree with all the views presented in articles within this Book "*Who Really Killed JFK (Facts & Theories)*". The author will always give opposing views equal treatment: you, the readers, are clever enough to decide who has the better arguments. The author exercises its sole discretion in determining to include whatever materials happen to strike his attention; stimulate the thoughts of, or enliven discussions among others; or which otherwise informs the public about issues which are related to the goals of informing the public. Frequently, the materials included within this book will represent more than one side of any given issue.

Accordingly, statements made within any documents or any other materials in any of these pages or anywhere else used to support the book "*Who Really Killed JFK (Facts & Theories)*" do not necessarily represent the views or opinions of anyone else at all, other than the author of the material in question. None of the authors, contributors, sponsors, administrators, Web Sites or anyone else connected with the research author is no way whatsoever can be responsible for the appearance of any inaccurate or libelous information or your use of the information contained in this book.

Therlee Gipson

Additional books can be viewed on **amazon.com/books.**
Just key in the author full name: Therlee gipson, or you can contact the author by other means for more information.

Thank You

Amazon. Com Books

Therlee Gipson (Author & Artist)
2027 Nottingham Place Allen, Texas 75013
Phone: (214)-383-4499   Cell: 972-365-1939
E-Mail: gtherlee@gmail.com

Google **Key in: Amazon. Com Books**

Search | Books | Therlee Gipson | Touch (Go)

Made in the USA
Charleston, SC
20 February 2016